# RON LYON & JENNY PASCHALL

**STANLEY PAUL**
LONDON

*To Fran, Arthur, Lynn, Gregory, Sascha, Ivana, Adam and Sara*
*who are all, in their own way, Beyond Belief!*

This edition first published in 1993

1 3 5 7 9 10 8 6 4 2

Copyright © Beyond Belief Limited 1993

The right of Ron Lyon and Jenny Paschall to be identified as the
authors of this book has been asserted by them in accordance with
the Copyright, Designs and Patents Act, 1988

First published in the United Kingdom in 1993 by
Stanley Paul & Company Limited
Random House, 20 Vauxhall Bridge Road, London SW1V 2SA

Random House Australia (Pty) Limited
20 Alfred Street, Milsons Point, Sydney, NSW 2061, Australia

Random House New Zealand Limited
18 Poland Street, Glenfield, Auckland 10, New Zealand

Random House South Africa (Pty) Limited
PO Box 337, Bergvlei, South Africa

Random House UK Limited Reg. No. 954009

ISBN 0 09 177983 9

Typeset by Textype Typesetters, Cambridge
Printed and bound in England by Clays Ltd, St Ives plc.

Front cover photographs:
*Above left*: Shark roof sculpture, Press Association
*Below left:* Skinned man by Fragonard, Beyond Belief Limited
*Centre:* 'Doc' Shiels performing levitation, Fortean Picture Library
*Below right:* Ruby the elephant, Phoenix Zoo (photo Dick George)
Back cover photographs:
*Top left:* Waterton owl creature, Beyond Belief Limited
*Centre left:* Worm charmers, Rex Features
*Below left:* Ben the pig at home, Rex Features
*Top right:* Best Store, Sacramento, Arcaid (photo Richard Bryant)

# Contents

# About the Authors

**RON LYON** is an award-winning producer/director whose achievements span the spectrum, from serious documentaries to successful movies for television. He has created and produced TV specials for the US National Educational Network and for ABC. In 1976 he teamed up with James T. Aubrey, former President of CBS and MGM to form Aubrey/Lyon Productions, and four years later Ron Lyon became President of Rastar Television. In this capacity, he acquired the vast collection of Robert Ripley's *Believe It or Not!* facts and oddities, created as ABC specials.

Their enormous success spawned the long-running series, with Ron Lyon based in Paris as Executive Producer. As this book goes to press, he is working on thirteen episodes of *Beyond Belief!* for Nickleodeon/MTV.

**JENNY PASCHALL** is Executive in Charge of Production on *Beyond Belief!*. Formerly an Executive in the advertising industry, she is an inveterate traveler and collector of odd facts and people. The most recent addition to her odd people collection is co-author Ron Lyon, to whom she is now married.

# Acknowledgements

The authors would like to thank the following people, all of whom helped to make this book possible: Jimmy Sangster, Mary Peach, John Kane, Kirk Schenck, Jack and Leonore Wax, Joel and Gladys Frederick, Roddy Bloomfield, Marion Paull, Claire Jenkinson, Michael Collyer, Sandy Carter, Jeremy Nussbaum, Andy Taylor, Aky Najeeb, Mike Miller, Bruce Dickinson and all at Sanctuary.

The author and publishers wish to thank the following for permission to reproduce photographs: Arcaid, pages 75 photo Richard Bryant and 86 photo Robert O'Dea; British Museum, London/Bridgeman Art Library, page 17 *right*; Civico Museo Correr, Venice/ Bridgeman Art Library, page 37; Bruce Coleman, pages 36 photo Hans Reinhard and 45 photo Peter Terry; Mary Evans Picture Library, pages 9, 11, 14, 16 *right*, 18, 28, 29, 30, 32 *left*, 33, 58, 68, 70, 77, 82, 83, 84, 87, 89 and 91 *left*; Fortean Picture Library, 34 and 38; Robert Harding Picture Library, pages 15 photo John Delorme, 71 and 76 photo Michael J. Howell; Harrods Limited, page 26; Michael Holford, page 16 *left*; Hulton Deutsch Collection, page 60; Imperial War Museum, pages 7, 49 and 95; Kobal Collection, pages 10, 20 and 24; Louvre, Paris/Bridgeman Art Library, page 8; Phoenix Zoo, page 50 *left* and *right* photos Dick George; Planet Earth Pictures, pages 35 photo Ron Bohr, 43 photo Flip Schulke, 46 photo Andre Bartschi, 47 photo Peter Scoones, 48 photo Pieter Folkens and 51 photo Jonathan Scott; Popperfoto, pages 31, 32 *riqht*, 41 *left* and *right*, 81, 85, 91 *right* and 93; Potter's Museum of Curiosity, page 13 *right*; Quadrant Picture Library, page 27; Rex Features, pages 53, 64, 65, 67 and 88; Science Photo Library, pages 23, 42 and 44; Wakefield Art Gallery, pages 12 and 13 *left*; Wellcome Institute Library, London, page 56.
All other photographs are the copyright of Beyond Belief Limited.

# Famous failures

In 1915 the British Admiralty ordered a submarine designed to run on steam. The boats were to be designated the K-series. By the time K-1 had been built its problems were apparent to everyone except the Naval authorities in charge of her design. The combination of the sub's 330 ft length and complicated handling made her cumbersome and temperamental. A crash dive in a K-boat took 5 minutes or more, compared with less than 2 minutes for a German U-boat.

During tests and maneuvers a fire broke out during K-2's first dive; K-3 nearly sank in Stokes Bay; K-4 hit a sandbar; K-5 and her crew of 57 disappeared. K-13 sank in Gairloch, Scotland: 32 men died.

In the first trial exercise which took place during January 1919 in Scotland K-14 was run down by K-22; K-22 was hit by the cruiser *Inflexible*; K-6 smashed into K-3 while trying not to hit K-4; K-17 collided with destroyer HMS *Fearless*; K-7, unable to turn quickly enough, plowed into K-17, which was already listing from the impact of *Fearless*.

That exercise was to be the K-boats' last. England's new submarines had resulted in death and destruction, but only for the 270 sailors who made up their crews.

**Convinced you've seen it all? In 1875 the Director of the United States Patent Office insisted that *he* had. He sent in his resignation, advising the administration that his department should be closed permanently. Why? He was convinced there was nothing left to invent.**

*K-2, pictured here under steam, began to go up in flames during her first dive.*

# Famous failures

The Marquis Eduardo de Valfierno was no ordinary con-man. In 1911 he devised a scheme to steal the 'Mona Lisa' and sell it, not once, but 6 times and to 6 different customers. He realized that there was a market for Da Vinci's masterpiece not amongst the world's art collectors, who displayed their treasures, but among robber barons and empire builders, to whom even clandestine ownership of such riches represented power.

Valfierno rented a studio and put Yves Chaudron, a talented profession-al forger, to work. Chaudron faithfully duplicated the enigmatic 'Mona Lisa' – 6 times over. The forgeries were then shipped to the United States of America.

Only then, with the fakes safely out of France, did Valfierno set out to steal the real thing. He recruited a small-time crook named Vincenzo Perugia. Dressed in workman's smocks, Perugia and his accomplice had no difficulty getting into the Louvre or taking the painting off the wall. Because the 'Mona Lisa' and other masterpieces were often removed and taken to a small studio within the museum to be photographed, no one questioned the thieves.

For Perugia, it was a good deal. Not only was Valfierno paying him but, as a bonus, he could even keep the painting. All Valfierno needed for his plan to work was for the world to know that the 'Mona Lisa' had been stolen, thus setting the stage for Valfierno to convince his covetous customers that he was delivering the authentic 'Mona Lisa', each customer would receive an original forgery. It was the perfect sting: a cheat cheating cheats. None of his customers could ever have their paintings authenticated by experts be-cause they would incriminate themselves if they did.

Valfierno allegedly made over 2 million dollars on the 6 deals. Perugia, the actual thief, made the mist-ake of trying to sell the original. He was arrested and went to jail. The real 'Mona Lisa' was return-ed safely to the Louvre. Valfierno continued his life of deception despite testimony by Perugia about his forgeries.

**As for the 6 millionaires who had been taken to the cleaners – they never said a word.**

The British seem to have been a little short-sighted when it came to innovations. In 1876, the British Post Office rejected the concept of the telephone on the grounds that, while the Americans might find a use for such a thing, the British had plenty of small boys who would run messages. The first telephone exchange was opened in Britain 3 years later. At about the same time, Sir William Preece, Chief Engineer of the British Post Office, heard about Edison's development of electric light. He declared it to be a completely idiotic idea. Perhaps there were enough small boys to hold candles too!

It has been said that criminal failures come in only one form: those who get caught when they never intended to! John Breads might cause us to think again. He got caught committing a crime he never intended. Breads had one simple goal: to kill James Lamb, the Mayor of Rye, in England, one night as the politician was on his way to a late dinner. But Lamb fell ill and sent a man by the name of Greable in his place. Because the night in question was cold Lamb lent Greable one of his trademark red coats.

Breads, the town butcher, followed the man in the red coat through the dark streets of Rye, caught up with him and stabbed the red coat repeatedly. Then, thinking he had killed the mayor, he ran through the town yelling, 'Butchers should stab lambs.' He was subsequently sentenced for his all-but self-confessed crime by his intended victim, the mayor.

Not surprisingly Breads was hanged. His body was encased in a gibbet and displayed in the town square. The actual gibbet can still be seen in Rye today. But of James Breads, bungling murderer, only the top of his skull remains. The rest of his bones were chipped away by villagers. According to local custom, they placed the chips of the criminal's skeleton in their soup – for good luck!

When Rudyard Kipling was dismissed from his position as a reporter with the *San Francisco Examiner*, his editor's parting words were '… you just don't know how to use the English language. This isn't a kindergarten for amateur writers.'

Horatio Alger (1832-1899) has become a symbolic representation of the modern American success story. He sold over 18 million copies of his rags-to-riches tales, making a fortune in the process. Unfortunately, he squandered or gave away most of his wealth and died broke. The real Horatio Alger story was very much a case of 'From Rags to Riches to Rags'.

**When Fred Astaire made his first screen test for MGM, the verdict was: 'Can't act, slightly bald, can dance a little'.**

In 1943, at the heart of World War II, Turkey was still neutral. All the international powers, including the British and Germans, maintained embassies in the Turkish capital, Ankara. While working as a driver at the British Embassy there, Elyesa Bazna was amazed at how casually the British treated secret papers, often leaving them in unlocked desks. He decided to make a career move: he would become valet to the Ambassador, Sir Hughe Knatchbull-Hugessen, and a spy for the German government.

While trying to assess which of the many documents would be the most valuable to the Germans, he discovered that when classified papers were not being used they were kept in locked vaults. At night some were removed from the vault, placed in a red box which was also locked, and taken by the Ambassador to his residence next door.

The dilemma of which of these papers was the most important was solved for Bazna by Sir Hughe, who took the most important papers from the red box, placed them in a black box, and took them to his bedroom to study. Only the Marx Brothers could have conceived a more convoluted scenario. For Bazna it became a simple matter of duplicating the Ambassador's key to the black box. Thereafter, every morning, while the Ambassador ate his breakfast, Bazna photographed the contents of the box.

He eventually contacted the German Embassy and struck a deal. He would receive £15,000 for every roll of film. Over a period of time he received more than a quarter of a million pounds. Included within the information given to the Germans was the approximate date and, even more important, the location of the planned Allied invasion of Europe. There was only one thing wrong with the report. It contradicted Hitler's conclusions about where the invasion would come and since Hitler considered himself to be the century's greatest military genius he ignored the documents supplied by Bazna.

Bazna waited until several years after the war to spend his fortune. He began to buy land but was immediately arrested, not for treason, but for passing counterfeit money. The Germans had paid him in phony currency. Elyesa Bazna, codenamed 'Cicero' by the Germans, had been duped. Unbelievably, when he was released by the Turkish authorities he sued the postwar German government for violation of contract and fraud. Some case. Elyesa Bazna, the daring master spy, ended his days working as a night watchman, the last act of this comedy of errors.

During an opening ceremony at the Kemper Arena in Kansas City the building's designer, Helmut Jahn, was to receive a citation from the president of the American Institute of Architects. A thousand of the world's most renowned architects had gathered inside the building for the event when the roof of the $20 million building fell in. As Frank Lloyd Wright said, 'The failed doctor can bury his mistakes, but the failed architect can only advise his client to plant vines.'

An unfortunate passenger traveling on the French TGV high-speed train from Paris to Toulouse dropped his wallet down the toilet. Naturally the man (who preferred to remain anonymous) tried to retrieve it – and wedged his hand firmly in the bowl in the process. He sounded the alarm and the train stopped near the town of Tours. The Fire Department was called in and metal cutters were used to extricate the passenger, and the toilet, from the train. The man was last seen by his fellow travelers lying on the station platform with the toilet wrapped around his arm. A case of being flushed with success? Perhaps not.

## Cézanne was turned down by the Ecole des Beaux-Arts when he applied for entrance.

Hans Christian Andersen's critics probably lived to eat their words. They insisted that his stories were 'quite unsuitable for children, positively harmful for the young mind'.

## Herman Melville became so disillusioned by the widespread failure of one of his novels that he gave up writing and became a clerk in the New York Customs House. It wasn't until many years after his death in 1891 that Melville's novels and short stories gained recognition. The failure which drove Melville from author to office worker was called *Moby Dick*.

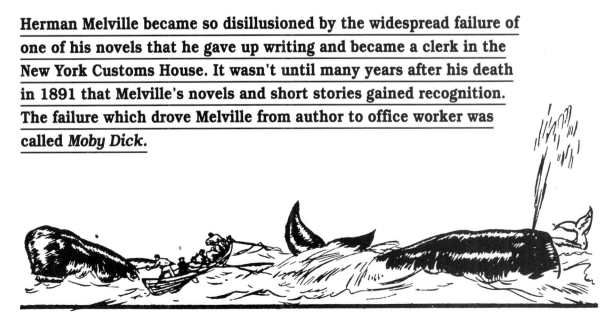

# Eccentrics

Waterton's
political creation 'John Bull and the
National Debt' showing the country as a porcupine
with a tortoiseshell and an almost human face so
weighed down by the National Debt of £800
million that it is being overcome by 6 devils.

Waterton Hall, near Wakefield, England, is the home of one of the most bizarre exhibits of taxidermy in the world. It forms part of the collection of Charles Waterton, a notable 19th-century naturalist, who spent most of his adult life traveling the world studying nature, particularly animal life. He also loved adventure. It is said he captured a boa constrictor with his bare hands, and wrestled with an alligator until he subdued it. As he grew older he gave up his travels and settled in Yorkshire, where he created the world's first bird and wild-animal sanctuary.

He took up taxidermy and, apparently bored with the commonplace, began to suture together the limbs and heads of different animals, producing weird 'new species'. He attached the legs and head of a lizard, mouth agape, teeth-bared, to a tortoiseshell, introducing it as an astounding discovery. He stitched an owl's head on the body of a rooster and created a simian mix with a quizzical expression frozen on its face.

Soon there were dozens of these creatures, each with a name reflecting Waterton's political opinions. One was called 'John Bull and the National Debt'. But it wasn't until he introduced 'The Nondescript' that he achieved international notoriety.

The Nondescript captured the imagination of everyone who saw it. It looked like a miniature man in a furry orange Eskimo hood. Waterton published a lengthy treatise about it, complete with engravings. He claimed that he had discovered a new species, an animal which would change our thinking about the natural world. He would not, however, explain how he had managed to capture it, or where it came from, claiming he had to protect his find from an inquiring and potentially dangerous academic world.

Professors of zoology and biology from universities around the world debated different theories about the Nondescript's origin. They visited, they gaped, they expounded. The creature bewildered them. A controversy of huge academic proportions ensued about its origins. The locals believed it was the head of a native, whom old Charlie had killed, brought back and stuffed. Some of them even said it looked suspiciously like the town's missing mailman.

Waterton had simply taken the head of a howling monkey, stretched its skin across a metal frame and given it a human expression. But he told no one about his deception. He had completed his journey from scholar to scoundrel.

As he grew older he developed paranoia. He was convinced that poachers were breaching the security of his walled estate to hunt or steal his animals. He took to hiding in the trees, lying in wait and then leaping down on to unsuspecting people. He would taunt them with a spear or other exotic mementos of his past until they ran off in terror. Sadly, this behavior was to be the end of old Charlie. After having wrestled alligators, strangled boa constrictors and slept in vampire-bat caves, Charles Waterton, at the age of 83, fell to his death from a tree.

*Waterton's Nondescript baffled experts around the world.*

Walter Potter would probably have enjoyed Charles Waterton's company. He created Potter's Museum of Curiosity, in Cornwall, in 1862. Potter was a talented but eccentric taxidermist. He believed that stuffed animals were a little dull so he dressed them in costumes and presented them in elaborate tableaux. His collection includes a kittens' tea party, in which 37 kittens, dressed in fashionable clothes, play croquet. The rabbits' school has 20 rabbits sitting at school desks. Potter also preserved freaks of nature, such as a 2-headed lamb and a goat with 6 legs.

*Walter Potter's kittens all dressed up for an elegant feline wedding.*

Henry Cope, of Brighton, England, was what one might call 'green', Every item of his clothing was green. His house, his stove, his furniture were green. His walking stick was green, his carriage was green, he even painted his horse green. He ate only green food. Perhaps worried that their 'green man' would begin covering the town with green paint or that *they* would all begin looking a bit green, the people of Brighton had him committed to an insane asylum for the rest of his life. Perhaps Henry Cope had discovered the secret of happiness, thereby making his neighbors green with envy. He might have been better off in Greenland!

French physician Alain Bombard was determined to prove that most deaths resulting from shipwrecks were caused by ignorance of basic survival techniques.

To test his theory he set off from the Canary Islands in 1952 to cross the Atlantic to the West Indies in a 15 ft rubber dingy. He took no food, water or general provisions. He did not accept the widely held hypothesis that drinking sea water leads to insanity and death.

During his voyage he was careful to drink a pint and a half of sea water each day. He ate raw fish, caught with a handmade harpoon, and to make sure he did not develop scurvy, he ate plankton, scooped from a net of closely-woven cloth which trailed from his boat.

After 53 days at sea Bombard was about to give up. Hailing a ship on the open seas, he discovered he was still 600 miles from land. But after a hearty meal he regained his bravado and sailed on. He reached Barbados on Christmas Eve, having drifted more than 2,650 miles in 65 days. He had lost almost 60 lb, but had survived to prove his point.

Mad Jack Fuller who lived in Sussex, England, in the early 19th century, loved both a good wager and practical jokes. This 300 lb Member of Parliament had a 65 ft-high stone obelisk built in the middle of a field. When one of his neighbors enquired, 'Jack, why?' Fuller's response was, 'Because it wasn't there.'

A 30 ft-high structure now called 'The Sugar Loaf of Dallington' was constructed for Fuller almost overnight. It seems he had mentioned in passing that he could see the spire of the local church from the porch of his home atop Rose Hill. A fellow parliamentarian overheard and bet Mad Jack to the contrary. Never one to turn down easy money, Jack accepted the bet, offering great odds. When he returned

Beau Brummell was the original Mr Clean – and a great trend-setter. Historically, the average person rarely bathed. King Louis XII of France once bragged that he had only bathed twice in his life. Even in the 19th century bathing was considered an aberration. Brummell changed this. Not only did he bathe a number of times a day, he also scrubbed every part of his body for hours before dressing.

He annoyed his friends by refusing to shake hands, tip his hat to the ladies or even turn his head at an angle to speak (he was more concerned about preserving the creases in his clothing and the parting in his hair). He even washed the soles of his shoes with champagne. He would change his clothes 3 times a day and every week have his entire wardrobe laundered in the country so that it would smell, in his words, 'like new-mown hay'.

to Rose Hill he realized that he had miscalculated. The church was in a valley and even if he climbed on to the roof of his house, he was unable to see it.

Mad Jack had to act quickly, because his friend was due to visit him within a few days. He assembled the local craftsmen and had them build a replica of the church spire so that it could be seen on the horizon when viewed from his house. By the time the bettor came to collect, the spire was clearly visible, enriching not only Jack but local folklore as well.

Among his other eccentricities, he once paid for a 6 ft-high wall nearly 4 miles long to be built for no apparent reason. The locals say it was to keep the stonemasons in Jack's district employed.

His greatest folly, however, was his last. In an arrangement with the local minister, he agreed to relocate a pub he owned from its position directly across the street from the church to 1 mile down the road. In exchange he was to be allowed to build the tomb of his choice in the churchyard. Fuller hired Sir Robert Smirke, architect of the British

*Mad Jack Fuller's hastily constructed obelisk won him a lucrative bet.*

**When one of his neighbors enquired, 'Jack, why?' Fuller's response was, 'Because it wasn't there.'**

Museum, to design and construct the mausoleum. Always larger than life, both in girth and in attitude, Fuller had Smirke design a two-story pyramid, with a chamber inside big enough for him to be buried sitting upright wearing a top hat, with a roast chicken and a bottle of good red wine on a table in front of him. Broken glass was to be scattered throughout to stop the devil from disturbing Jack's eternal feast.

The pyramid was constructed, taking a good proportion of the graveyard and competing for attention with the tiny country church itself.

For years after Mad Jack's death in 1834 his monument in Brightling churchyard was a subject of controversy. There was even talk of replacing it with a more discreet memorial. It was decided to open the tomb and see how Mad Jack was doing. The tomb was empty! No table, no chicken, no wine, no top hat – and no Jack Fuller: it was Mad Jack's final joke. He built the most talked about tomb in the country and he wasn't even in it.

The pyramid can still be seen preserved in the Brightling church-yard today. As for Mad Jack, he's probably still having a good laugh – somewhere.

# Eccentrics

Jeremy Bentham, the father of utilitarianism and one of the founders of the University of London in the UK, could be considered the eccentric's eccentric. He left his entire estate to University College on condition that he be publicly dissected in front of his friends, then stuffed, dressed in his finest clothes and mounted in a chair. He ordered that his walking stick, which he affectionately called 'Dapple', be placed in his hand.

His will also stipulated that he must continue to attend the annual meeting of the University's Board of Governors. Therefore, ever since his death in 1832 his remains have attended these meetings. He is listed as 'present, but not voting'. Where there's a will there's a way...

*Dead but not forgotten: Jeremy Bentham's stuffed body still attends University meetings.*

In 1701, as an alternative to going to Debtors' Prison, Edward Hide Cornbury, third Earl of Clarendon, became Governor of New York and New Jersey. It was an experience for which the Colonies could not have been prepared.

Cornbury, a man of excesses and eccentricities, outdid himself when he arrived at the Governor's Ball in a stunning dress made especially for the occasion and accompanied by his wife wearing complementary colors. Thereafter Cornbury more often than not dressed in ladies' clothes *à la mode* and began addressing his assemblies on the virtues of the female anatomy – specifically his wife's – rather than the problems of the day.

An obsessive fondler, he could not keep his hands off anyone. Frequently, unsuspecting males were the recipients of his manual attentions. While graft and bribes kept him in money, Queen Anne kept him in gowns.

By 1708 the Colonists had seen enough. He was removed from office and jailed by his creditors. However, his father conveniently died, leaving him the title of Earl of Clarendon and freeing him from prosecution. Queen Anne immediately recalled him to England, where he continued to live up to his reputation as an eccentric. Perhaps he spent the rest of his life as a Lady in Waiting...

# Odd bods

Members of the Hare family were lords of Stow Bardolf manor in Norfolk for hundreds of years. Stone and marble effigies of many of them can still be seen in the local church of the Holy Trinity, which dates from 1189. Perhaps the most bizarre memorial belongs to Lady Sarah Hare. Legend has it that while sewing one a Sunday, a sacrilegious practice in the 1700s, Sarah accidentally pricked herself on the finger with a needle. She died soon afterwards.

Her husband had a wax figure of her placed in a mahogany case in the family chapel. It can still be seen, dressed in the clothes she died in. You could say she is the 'Hare' apparent to the legend of Sleeping Beauty. However, looking at her effigy it's easy to understand why she hasn't been kissed by anyone in the last 250 years.

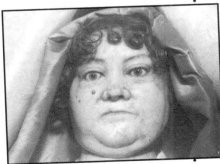

Sir Walter Raleigh's widow had some interesting ornaments laying around the house, not the least of which was her husband's head. After his execution by Queen Elizabeth I his body was buried near the altar of a church in Westminster. His head was placed in a red velvet bag and given to his widow. She had it preserved and displayed in her home. Many years later when their son died he left instructions that the head be buried with him but unfortunately it had somehow disappeared. Sir Walter is possibly the only man to lose his head twice.

To the tenth Duke of Hamilton, dying was no laughing matter. In fact, he felt it would be a joke for his aristocratic bones to be buried in a conventional coffin. So, outbidding the British Museum, he bought a sarcophagus thought to have belonged to an Egyptian princess.

The Duke's dreams of being buried like royalty were soon to become a nightmare. As he lay dying, it was brought to his attention that his glorified resting chamber was too short – by 1 ft. To this the Duke replied, 'Well then, double me up!'

After he died, however, it soon became apparent that his stiff, rather rotund body was not going to double up as he had envisioned. In order to place him in his prized sarcophagus, it was necessary to cut off his feet.

A short time afterwards the British Museum notified the Duke's estate that the sarcophagus, was *not* formerly that of an Egyptian princess at all, but of a court jester – who seems to have had the last laugh on the old Duke.

# Odd bods

Honoré Fragonard (a relative of the artist) trained as a veterinarian. In 1766 he was appointed Lecturer of Anatomy at the Paris Veterinary School. While there, he began anatomical research which stressed the physician's need to get below the surface of medical problems, his studies eventually forming the basis of his work *Précis Anatomique du Corps du Cheval*. During his many procedures Fragonard developed a way of preserving deceased humans and animals after removing – their skin. He managed to retain the muscles and blood vessels in place as if the skin were still holding them together.

Not surprisingly, he was a controversial

*Fragonard, the vet who got under people's skin.*

figure, regarded with suspicion by most of his contemporaries, though it is uncertain whether they disapproved of his work or simply feared that they might end up the subject of one of his experiments.

Not long after Fragonard's fiancée died, her body was stolen from its grave. Subsequently Fragonard presented his *Cavalier Anatomisé*, a perfect human body, skinned and preserved, astride a skinless, galloping horse. Some say the rider is the missing fiancée. Surrounded by other similarly macabre specimens, both flayed horse and rider can still be seen at the Maison-Alfort near Paris, frozen in a bizarre gallop across eternity.

**If anyone went digging for gold beneath the Bank of England, they might unearth instead – a giant. An 8 ft giant named Jenkins asked to be buried there to protect him from body snatchers. When he died in 1798 his request was granted.**

In 1983, 2 men digging in a field in Cheshire, England, unearthed the remains of a human body. They assumed that the well-preserved corpse had been buried recently. The coroner pronounced it to be the body of a woman aged about 35. She had been strangled – the cord was still round her neck. The police had no suspects.

After reading about the case a man named Peter Bardt, believing the body to be that of his wife, confessed that he had murdered her in 1960. He was tried, found guilty and imprisoned. At the time no one knew that 12 other bodies had been found in similar circumstances: in Norway, Ireland, Denmark, Germany and another in England. All had died violently. Some had been strangled with a noose, 2 had had their throats cut, 2 had been decapitated. All the bodies were found in the same bog-like ground but apart from Peter Bardt's wife, none was identifiable. Eventually the authorities realized that Mrs Bardt had never actually been identified. Her husband had confessed to her murder, but at no time did he see the body. So they examined it again, but in more detail, and using sophisticated methods. Tests were made to ascertain exactly how long it had been buried. It was then that it became clear a mistake had been made. This body, like the other 12 found across Europe, had been killed in approximately 210 AD. The bodies had been preserved by the soil in which they were buried.

As for Peter Bardt, he is serving a life sentence for confessing to a crime committed over 1,700 years earlier – proving the adage 'Fish get hooked by their mouths'.

Paula Beswick, of Willey, in Shropshire, England, left a fortune to her physician on condition that he look upon her face once a year as long as he lived. The physician decided to honor this request in a way that would cause him little inconvenience: he had her body embalmed and kept it in the case of a grandfather clock.

**Willie Stokes, of Chicago, Illinois, had some definite ideas about *his* last resting place too. He was buried in a custom-made coffin which looked exactly like a Cadillac Seville, complete with steering wheel and tyres.**

When Mrs Martin Van Butchell died in 1775 her will mandated that her husband was not to receive his large inheritance unless her body remained above ground. Accordingly he had her embalmed, dressed her in her finest clothing and put her on display in the family parlor, holding daily visiting hours for her former friends.

Word spread of Mrs Van Butchell's impressive condition and embalming became popular. Undertakers skilled in the art created a thriving business for themselves by touring their prize corpses, displaying them in shop windows, at county fairs and in music-hall lobbies.

# Odd bods

June Mathis was a plain woman, who made a living translating classic novels and plays into silent movies. During the preparation of one screen treatment, she met and fell in love with a young Rodolpho di Valentina. She arranged for him to be cast in the featured role in *The Four Horsemen of the Apocalypse* and, once production had begun, she expanded the role far beyond what was originally intended.

Rudolf Valentino became a star and June Mathis was happy to devote her life to him and his career. She followed him from Metro Pictures to Adolph Zukor's Famous Players and eventually created the role of 'The Sheik' for him. She watched as women came into, and went out of, his life, without having a romantic relationship with him herself.

When Valentino died suddenly at the age of 31 his family had made no provisions for his burial, so June took control, providing him with a crypt at Hollywood Memorial Cemetery. Only 10 months after his death June Mathis also died. Her will set out her finally wishes, the wishes of her lifetime: she was to be buried next to her idol in the unoccupied space adjacent to his crypt.

The woman who rests by Valentino is not a famous beauty, nor one of his wives or many lovers. She is a plain little lady who wrote screen treatments but she will, for eternity, sleep with the greatest screen lover of all time.

*Valentino took Agnes Ayres into his arms - no such luck for June Mathis*

Jimmy Dale Stubble, a cowboy from Grand Junction, Colorado, was paralyzed from the neck down after a fight with another cowboy. Having spent so much of his life in a wheelchair, he decided, when he died, to be buried standing up. His friends dressed him in full cowboy regalia and his saddle-draped coffin was lowered, feet first, into the ground. For those who attended the ceremony it was Stubble's Last Stand.

During October 1888 a series of ghastly discoveries was made in London. First, a severed arm was found in the Thames. Then, one afternoon a carpenter named Frederick Wildborn found a neatly wrapped parcel in the building site where he was working. It contained the trunk of a woman. Police confirmed that the arm found earlier belonged to this body, along with another arm discovered in another part of the city. The dismembered body was found on the building site of Scotland Yard, the new headquarters of London's élite police force. The murder victim was never identified and the murderer never found. Scotland Yard has never been able to solve a murder that took place in 'its own backyard'.

When beheading became the preferred means of sealing an aristocrat's fate in Revolutionary Europe, the ancient custom of laying a deceased relative to rest in their bed for viewing presented something of a problem. Faced with this dilemma, relatives could either pull the sheets up to the chin or sew the head back on to the body. They chose the latter. In many posthumous portraits the stitches can be seen on the once severed neck. Not a pretty sight.

One of the first things Oliver Cromwell did when he overthrew the British monarchy in the 17th century was to have King Charles I beheaded and the head paraded around London on a wagon cart.

Cromwell named himself Lord Protector of England and began weeding out enemies of the state, starting with members of the Royal Family. After 5 years as absolute dictator he died peacefully in his bed. His body was embalmed, a lavish state funeral took place and he was interred in Westminster Abbey, London.

Two years later Charles II, son of Charles I, restored the monarchy. He had Cromwell's body exhumed and dragged through the streets of London to Tyburn, where it was publicly hanged on the gallows, then beheaded. It took the slipshod executioner 8 strokes of his axe to complete the deed. In the process, he damaged Cromwell's nose as well as some other vital parts of his anatomy. Spiked on a pole, the disfigured head was paraded through the streets and finally housed on the roof of the House of Commons.

One night 24 years later, during a particularly heavy storm, a sentry was almost knocked out by what he thought was a cannon ball falling from the sky. In fact, he had been hit by Cromwell's head, which had been shaken loose by the wind. The sentry wrapped up the head and took it home, selling it eventually to an itinerant, who went from village to village, charging people to see it, or, for a higher fee, to hold it. For the next 200 years it was exhibited in peep shows. In the end it made its way back to Cambridge, Cromwell's alma mater. There, remarkably well preserved, although now missing an ear as well as the nose, it was placed in an oak box and, in a final ceremony in 1960, laid to rest at his old college, Sydney Sussex. As for the rest of his body, perhaps that, too, will turn up some day.

# Odd bods

In 1737, when Galileo's body was being moved for final burial in Florence, a nobleman named Anton Francesco Gori cut off 3 of Galileo's fingers to keep as relics. As a result, while most of Galileo is buried in Florence next to Michelangelo and Machiavelli, his middle finger is on display in Florence's Museum of the History of Science and the remaining 2 are now in a private collection.

In the days before medical techniques were developed to determine brain death, a society was formed for the Prevention of People Being Buried Alive. Fearful that someone falling into a coma or other state simulating death could be buried but then regain consciousness, the society devised an alarm system utilizing a bell and a piece of string. The ill-fated and, one would suspect, bewildered victim could thus summon help. The society's last known member was buried over 100 years ago. As no one has heard from him since, it can be assumed he was a dead ringer.

Joseph Haydn spent his most prolifically creative years in Eisenstadt, Austria, working under the patronage of the Prince of Esterhazy.

He died in Vienna but his grateful master had his body returned to Eisenstadt for burial in a suitably grand marble tomb. However, a group of phrenologists wanted to study Haydn's skull in the hope of discovering the root of his great talent. Accordingly, his body was removed from its temporary resting place and decapitated.

The culprit refused to return the head until Prince Esterhazy compensated him. The Prince would not be blackmailed so Haydn's body was reburied headless.

The head was eventually bequeathed to the Musikverein museum, in Vienna, but it disappeared again. It then reappeared at the home of an Austrian professor, who displayed it on his piano. When the professor died, his widow loaned the head to the Vienna Pathological Museum. The Musikverein sued for its return. It was returned in 1895 and remained in Vienna while the people of Eisenstadt negotiated, for over 40 years, to have it back and put in the tomb.

Then came World War II. In 1945, with Haydn's head now in the Russian Sector of a divided Vienna, discussions began again.

It was not until 1954, 145 years after his death, that Joseph Haydn's head was finally reunited with his body.

Three old buildings in Hong Kong make up the most bizarre hotel in the world. Although it has at any given time up to 300 residents it offers no amenities or services, has no baths and no telephones. Yet year in, year out it runs at almost full occupancy.

Who stays? Deceased Chinese citizens who want to be buried in their ancestral home, in this case mainland China. It is in their homeland that Fengshui (wind and water) exists. Fengshui are the spiritual laws which govern yin and yang, the male-female elements in nature.

The 'hotel' was created in 1899 in order to ensure burial in the land of favorable Fengshui. Since land is expensive and the wait for a plot can be lengthy, people rent space for their coffins either in halls or in single or double rooms. When space becomes available on the mainland, the guests are transported to their final resting place. In the meantime they are in residence in Tung Wah Coffin Home.

How's the service? Thus far, no complaints.

# Body parts

Physicians insist that bathing the body on a daily basis is crucial to maintain proper dermatological hygiene. However, some people find bathing in mere water to be a bit dull. They prefer to soak in mud, Jell-O or a concoction of orange peels. The Japanese often bathe in flowers, while in 1986 a man named Barry Kirk bathed in a vat of baked beans for 100 hours. Not to be outdone, a man named Peter Smart bathed in a tub of 2 million maggots for 24 hours! Peter Smart must know something we don't.

**If translated into print, the genetic information contained in a single human DNA molecule would easily fill 500 telephone directories.**

The kidney of the average human being consists of millions of microscopic tubes. Stretched end to end, the total length of these tubes would be over 50 miles.

Our stomachs are filled with hydrochloric acid, an integral part of the human digestive process. This substance is such a concentrated corrosive that it can eat its way through a cotton towel and even through the paint and body of a car. Remarkably, it cannot penetrate the lining of the stomach, which is protected by a thin film of adhesive mucus impervious to the acid. It's a good thing we don't have cast iron stomachs.

*A head louse clinging to a hair - just one of many creepy creatures in residence on the human body.*

You can't see them, but they're there, in your skin: bacteria, mites, yeasts and the like, which take residence on our skin on a daily basis. There are as many as 5,000 little creepy-crawlers crowded into every square centimeter of a forearm. And as if that's not bad enough, there are more bugs and other living creepies on the skin of the average human being than there are humans on earth. Scientists have not yet summoned the courage to research the number of creatures which may inhabit our armpits – so those figures may soon need to be adjusted.

The only part of the human body that does not receive a supply of blood is the cornea. It receives its oxygen nourishment directly from its contact with the air.

# Alchemists

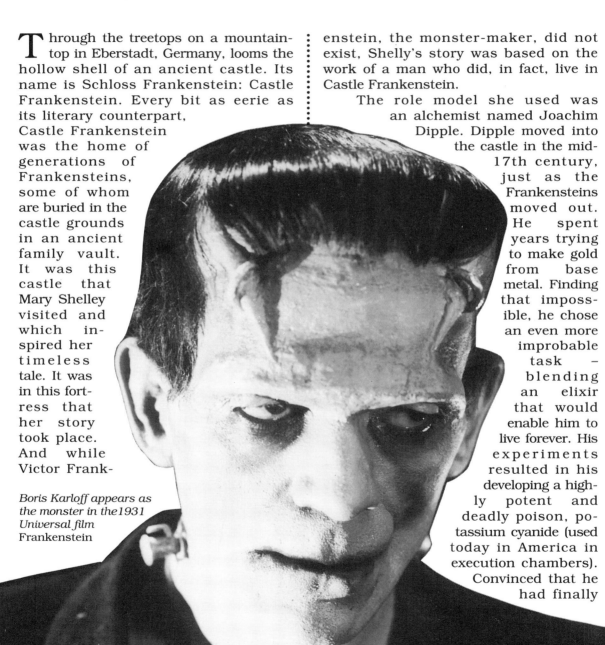

Through the treetops on a mountaintop in Eberstadt, Germany, looms the hollow shell of an ancient castle. Its name is Schloss Frankenstein: Castle Frankenstein. Every bit as eerie as its literary counterpart, Castle Frankenstein was the home of generations of Frankensteins, some of whom are buried in the castle grounds in an ancient family vault. It was this castle that Mary Shelley visited and which inspired her timeless tale. It was in this fortress that her story took place. And while Victor Frank-

*Boris Karloff appears as the monster in the 1931 Universal film* Frankenstein

enstein, the monster-maker, did not exist, Shelly's story was based on the work of a man who did, in fact, live in Castle Frankenstein.

The role model she used was an alchemist named Joachim Dipple. Dipple moved into the castle in the mid-17th century, just as the Frankensteins moved out. He spent years trying to make gold from base metal. Finding that impossible, he chose an even more improbable task – blending an elixir that would enable him to live forever. His experiments resulted in his developing a highly potent and deadly poison, potassium cyanide (used today in America in execution chambers). Convinced that he had finally discovered the secret of life, Joachim drank a healthy – well, perhaps not so healthy – dose of the liquid. Poor Joachim. In his search for the secret of life, he found only death.

As for Mary Shelley, she quickly realized that she could not call her monster-maker Dipple, so she called him Frankenstein. After all, who would be afraid of a 'Dipple Monster'?

At one time alchemists dreamt of creating gold out of everyday household waste. Today oil is often referred to as 'black gold'. And, in a way, Lonnie Ingram may be considered the first successful alchemist. In 1992 he received US Patent No. 5,000,000 for his custom-tailored microbe, which he affectionately refers to as 'Superbug'.

Ingram was trying to figure out how bacteria create tequila when he took 2 genes from one strain of bacteria and transferred them to another. The hybrid he developed turned out to be a ravenous bacterium that eats any kind of plant material: cornstalks, sawdust, grass clippings, old newspapers – even the sludge from paper mills.

What makes this living garbage disposal so valuable? Ingram realized that this invention was as good as gold when he discovered how this marvelous microbe was capable of turning waste into ethanol, a gas which scientists feel could replace oil-based fuels for use in automobiles. What's more, as a pure fuel, ethanol produces very little pollution. Essentially, Superbug may not only power tomorrow's car, it may also help to clean up the environment by eating the waste of so many other, less efficient, industrial processes.

In 1884, Harry Fell received a patent for a process in which he claimed he could turn wheat into gold. He thought it would make him a fortune. The process entailed placing carefully cut straw in water, letting it soak for a period, than straining off the liquid on top to collect the gold. Surprisingly, the British Patent Office granted him a patent on this process. Not surprisingly, Fell died broke. Maybe he had reached his last straw.

Diamonds are a girl's best friend – or used to be. Soon, if the Sewerage Bureau of Tokyo is to be believed, women will be longing for sewage! Due to a lack of land for fertilizer, disposal waste sludge is being used to make jewelry. The sludge is dried and heated to 1,400°C to produce a polished brown stone, which is then tastefully set into rings and pendants. Somehow, saying 'I love you' with recycled sewage seems to lack romance.

**John Rothman, creator of PooPets in Lancaster County, Pennsylvania, takes fresh bull manure, mixes and kneads then sculpts creatures such as Turdles, Stool Toads and Dung Bunnies to make the ultimate in environmentally friendly ornaments.**

A company called DejaShoe, in the United States, is taking recycling very seriously. They are making shoes with soles made of scrap rubber, tops from recycled cotton canvas, logo patch and molded back from recycled milk cartons, styrofoam coffee cups and lunch trays, innersoles from cardboard boxes, file folders and coffee filters and interfacing from recycled plastic soda bottles.

# Inventors

The first automobile was invented by Nicholas Cugnot in France, in 1771. It was a two-geared affair that ran on steam power and resembled a giant tea kettle. On its trial run the iron monster ran perfectly for the first few minutes but when Cugnot increased the speed, he lost control and crashed into a stone

wall. Although only his ego was bruised, Cugnot retired his machine. The 'car' can still be seen at the National Conservatory of Arts and Crafts in Paris.

## Thomas Edison made a fortune when he invented the lightbulb, but almost lost it by investing in cement furniture.

You can't make a silk purse out of a sow's ear – or can you? Researchers working in the laboratories of Arthur D. Little, an industrial research firm in Cambridge, Massachusetts, set out to prove that you can. A form of glue was extruded from the skin and gristle of a sow's ear, filtered, then placed on a spinneret and forced through a tube into a mixture of formaldehyde and acetone. The glue was further hardened by formaldehyde and combined with other streams into a single composite fiber. After a soaking in dyed glycerine, the resulting silk-like thread was woven into a Middle Ages-style lady's purse on a hand loom. They admitted, however, that the purse has no industrial or commercial value!

When the first escalator was installed in Harrods, the elegant London department store, the ride was not only bumpy, but was also, for some of its users, decidedly precarious. Instead of encouraging people to go from one floor to the next, the new invention frightened them away. So the management decided to serve brandy free of charge to any passengers who felt faint when they reached the top. It is reported that a steady stream of customers soon began using the new-fangled contraption – and feeling faint, time and time again! The escalator was a success.

*A tipple revived shoppers frightened of toppling!*

In 1923 the Rev J.G.P. Crawford, of Saunderstown, Rhode Island, invented the micropantograph, a machine which can write the Lord's Prayer within a space smaller than the eye of a needle. As many as 70 or 80 messages of 56 words can be inscribed on a surface the size of a grain of rice. The micropantograph was designed to send secret wartime messages. A machine can still be seen at the Smithsonian, in Washington.

The cigarette lighter was invented by J.W. Dobereiner in 1816 – before the match. Unfortunately, the German chemist's invention did not prove financially viable, because it needed powdered platinum to act as a catalyst – a very expensive smoke! The much more practical match was invented soon after-wards.

In 1937 the American cartoonist E.C. Segar introduced a creature called Eugene the Jeep as Popeye's trusty, go-anywhere pal. Jeeps, according to the cartoon strip, were tough little animals who lived on orchids and could become invisible.

When a few years later the Willys company of Ohio won a US military contract to produce a powerful open-topped four seat vehicle, soldiers in Europe eventually gave it the name JEEP. America's most popular military vehicle was named after an invisible orchid eater. It could have been called the Willys 'Eugene'.

England did not take kindly to the motor-car, which frightened both people and horses. Police and magistrates waged a war against the offensive machines, which they considered noisy, dangerous and dirty. Speed traps were set up as early as 1902. Policemen would hide behind hedges with a bicycle and stop watch and fine or jail the offending motorist. One early speed merchant, Lord Montague of Beaulieu, was traveling on a deserted highway when he received a police summons for driving in excess of 12 mph, slower than a horse can gallop.

*Caught for speeding – by a policeman on foot!*

**The first traffic light was installed in England in 1868 in front of the Houses of Parliament. It was intended to manage the flow of thousands of pedestrians who passed through the area each day.**

# Inventors

In the 18th century Dom Pérignon, a monk at the Abbaye d'Hautvillers, in France, was in charge of making still Champagne at the Abbey. He had a theory that by fermenting it he could create a sparkling wine. But in order to prove his hypothesis he had to find an effective seal for the bottle to replace the wood and leather stopper commonly used. He had to go to Spain to find the answer: the cork. Thus equipped, he returned to France, successfully locked the bubbles in the bottles and created Champagne. When he drank his first glass he said, 'I am drinking the stars.' Perhaps more remarkable than his invention is the fact that for most of his life, Dom Pérignon was virtually blind.

**The first spectacles were invented in Pisa, Italy, by an unknown artisan in the year 1296. The first contact lens was conceived by Leonado da Vinci in the 15th century.**

New worlds were opened to the blind when Louis Braille invented his system of reading. Now, Ray Kurzweil has taken reading for the blind to new heights. The Kurzweil Reading Machine reads printed material *aloud*. Listeners can even choose from a variety of voices. The machine uses an electronic camera to scan printed material. It feeds the images into a mini-computer which recognizes each letter, groups the letters into words, then computes the pronunciation and stress and immediately produces a synthetic version of human speech.

James Puckle, inventor of the Puckle Gun, took a curious view of killing the enemy. For firing at Christians, his Puckle Gun could be loaded with conventional, round bullets. These were considered more humane and less painful than the ammunition for use against non-Christians. For the latter the Puckle Gun was to fire square bullets. After tests the gun was rejected, not only because it was impractical, but because it also conflicted with the British sense of fair play on the battlefield.

Probably no other aspect of our world is more universal than the observance of time. Six hundred years ago the few clocks that existed were accurate to within an hour a day. Today twin atomic hydrogen masers, installed in 1964 at the US Naval Research Laboratory in Washington DC, derive their time by monitoring the frequency of the hydrogen atom's transition period of 1,420,450,751,694 cycles/sec – which produces an accuracy to within 1 second every 1.7 million years. Not that any of us will be around to check!

In 1817 British authorities were so fed up with thievery at the Portsmouth Dockyard that they offered a reward to anyone who could come up with an inexpensive, yet impenetrable lock. Jeremiah Chubb was the winning designer. To test his lock the British government gave it to an imprisoned safecracker and offered him a full pardon if he could open it. After trying for 10 weeks, he finally gave up. Chubb's lock, which employed 6 control levers that had to be raised to an exact height by a key, has not been picked yet!

In the first half of the 19th century chefs often kept weapons in the kitchen, not to defend themselves but to open cans. The sealed metal container for food was introduced in England in 1812 but its designer failed to produce a device to get the food out. Consequently it took hatchets, hammers and sometimes guns to blast out the contents. The first can opener made its welcome appearance in 1860, after which the need for small arms in the kitchen soon disappeared.

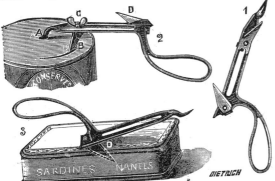

**Outils pour ouvrir les boîtes de conserves.** — Voici de nouveaux outils qu'il faudra bientôt utiliser pour ouvrir les boîtes de conserves. L'appareil, représenté dans le n° 1, permet d'ouvrir les boîtes rondes ainsi que les boîtes ovales ou carrées ; il est formé uniquement de deux tiges présentant une glissière dans laquelle on peut fixer les couteaux.

Outils pour boîtes de conserves. — 1. L'outil. — 2. Mode d'ouverture des boîtes rondes. — 3. Mode d'ouverture des boîtes carrées.

Un manche spécial recourbé se trouve à la suite. Pour les boîtes rondes (n° 2), on pique la pointe en A, au centre de la boîte ; on ajuste le couteau B à l'aide de la vis C ; on enfonce le couteau et on tourne en exerçant une légère pression. Pour les boîtes carrées (n° 3), il suffit d'enfoncer le couteau D et ... outils se trouvent chez M. Ma-

**The first false teeth were carved from the teeth of various mammals by the Etruscans around 700 BC in Italy – pity the Etruscan who lost a front tooth in a bat cave. This 'animal transplant' style of denture was popular until as late as the 19th century.**

Automata have been around since 2000 BC – both the Egyptians and the Greeks were fascinated by them. Louis XII of France owned a mechanical lion, made for him by Leonardo da Vinci. Charles V of Italy was so fascinated by automata that even when he developed religious mania and entered a monastery, he took his collection with him.

In 1774, Cox's Mechanical Museum in London exhibited the Silver Swan. A life-size working model, the graceful bird curves its long neck to plunge its head down to a lake of glass rods, and seizes a silver fish in its beak. This elegant routine is accompanied by music played on a set of bells. The swan can be seen in the Bowes Museum, in County Durham, England, where it is maintained in playing condition and operates once or twice a day.

**Sometimes the hand that feeds you can also pack quite a wallop. Madame Curie achieved fame by discovering radiation. That's the hand. Ironically, she was the first person to die from radiation poisoning. That's the wallop.**

# Royalty

**Emperor Norton was San Francisco's most popular tourist attraction in the 1870s. The *New York Times* called him 'Emperor of the World'.**

Did the United States ever have its own royalty? Yes. His name was Joshua Abraham Norton. His title? Emperor of the United States and Protector of Mexico. When did he reign? From 1859 to 1880.

Joshua Norton was a businessman, who had gone to San Francisco in the 1800s during the Gold Rush. By working as an agent, broker and land speculator, he made a fortune. At one point he cornered the market on rice, hoarded it and drove the price sky high. Then, suddenly, a competitor arrived in San Francisco with a shipload of rice from South America. The price of rice plummeted and Norton was ruined. He paid off his debts and disappeared.

When he reappeared, several years later, in September 1859 he was shabbily dressed in a Colonel's uniform. He marched into the offices of the *San Francisco Bulletin* and handed the editor the following proclamation, demanding that it be published in the paper the following day:

'At the peremptory request and desire of a large majority of the citizens of these United States I, Joshua Abraham Norton, declare and proclaim myself Emperor of these United States.' Astonishingly, the paper ran the declaration, and the reign of the Emperor Norton began. The citizens of San Francisco were happy to accept him as their Emperor. They would bow whenever he passed by, apparently enamored of his audacity as well as his bearing. Norton even delved into matters of state. He drafted several letters to President Lincoln, assuring him that while he was busy with the Civil War, Norton would watch over things. Ever the politician, to assure his subjects of his neutrality in the divisive War he wore a Union Army coat and a Confederate navy hat. He also solved his financial crisis. He simply began printing his own money, which he convinced merchants all around town to accept as legal tender. When he became bored with that, he levied taxes.

Throughout his reign he ate in restaurants, drank in bars and rode the trains and streetcars free of charge. Theaters even reserved special seats for him. He maintained this position for 20 incredible years, during which his loyal subjects in San Francisco shared his fantasy.

Visitors bought picture postcards of

Norton I, Emperor Norton dolls, and colored lithographs of the Emperor to hang in Victorian parlors. Tradesmen displayed signs in their windows to boast that they enjoyed his Royal Patronage.

When he died in 1880 thousands of people marched in his funeral procession and the city buried him with honors in a millionaire's grave. To this day an annual party is held in the cemetery on the anniversary of his death. And why not? Unlike most of history's kings, queens and emperors he never waged war or raised taxes. And he was good for business. What more could be asked of monarchy?

The world's heaviest living king is Tuafa'ahau of Tonga. In September 1976 the 6 ft 3 in monarch weighed himself on the only scale in his nation which could accommodate his bulk: the airport freight scale. He weighed 462 lb. By 1985 he was reported to have slimmed down by nearly 150 lb. His embassy car in London, England, bears the license plate '1 TON'.

## Versailles, the extravagant palace built by France's Louis XIV, has over 2,000 rooms, but not a single indoor toilet for a royal flush.

A well-respected astrologer once told the young King Louis XVI of France to beware the 21st day of each month. For the rest of his life he lived in fear of that dreaded day and avoided making plans or contact with people as far as possible. Come the revolution, Louis lost control of his appointment with death. He was arrested on the 21st, he lost his kingdom on the 21st, and was later executed at 10.22 am on January 21, 1793.

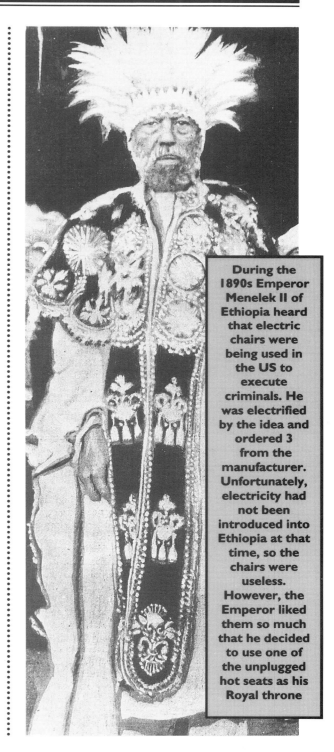

During the 1890s Emperor Menelek II of Ethiopia heard that electric chairs were being used in the US to execute criminals. He was electrified by the idea and ordered 3 from the manufacturer. Unfortunately, electricity had not been introduced into Ethiopia at that time, so the chairs were useless. However, the Emperor liked them so much that he decided to use one of the unplugged hot seats as his Royal throne

*Queen Victoria, the epitome of all things English, ruled for 64 years but never spoke fluent English: German was her first language.*

**Queen Berengaria, wife of Richard I of England, not only didn't speak English but also never managed to set foot on English soil during the whole of her reign.**

The Holy Roman Emperor Charlemagne was buried in 814 AD sitting on a marble chair with a crown on his head, a globe in one hand, a scepter in the other and an imperial robe over his shoulders.

King Umberto of Italy was dining in an elegant restaurant one night when he spotted a man who was practically his double. He called the man over and learned that he had been born on the same day in the same town as this mysterious man, that he had also married a woman named Marguerita on the same day and that they both had sons named Vittorio. The King was so amazed that he decided to bestow an honor on him. But, unfortunately the next day he learned that his mirror image had been gunned down in a fight earlier that morning. That same day King Umberto was killed by an assassin.

*Spot the difference: which is the real Umberto?*

George I, King of Great Britain and Ireland from 1714 to 1727, was born in Germany, spent most of his reign in Hanover, and didn't speak a word of English. Queen Victoria was brought up speaking German at home. Although she ruled England for 64 years and is probably one of the best known of all English monarchs, she never spoke English fluently.

In 1355 a macabre ceremony took place in the Portuguese city of Coimbra. It was the result of the unfortunate occurrences that followed the discovery of Prince Pedro of Aragon's secret marriage to the Castilian Princess Ines Piras de Castro. Ines had gone to Portugal in 1342 to be lady-in-waiting to Pedro's wife-to-be. When Pedro's father, King Alfonso of Portugal, learned of the marriage he had Ines brutally murdered.

Pedro had his revenge when he became king 2 years later. He ordered that his wife's assassins' hearts be ripped from their bodies. Then he had her decaying corpse exhumed and dressed in royal robes. This was followed by a full coronation ceremony, after which she was seated on a throne next to her King. His final reprisal was to order all the members of his court to come forward, one by one, pledge their allegiance to Queen Ines and kiss her rotting hand. In death, Queen Ines of Portugal had her vengeance.

**After 20 years as the faithful unpaid servant of the Duke of Windsor, Walter Monckton was rewarded with a cigarette case with his name beautifully engraved – but mis-spelt! Let's hope he knew it's the thought that counts.**

The guest list for dinner at Buckingham Palace can total 200, or more. Since all the guests must be served the same courses at the same time, hundreds of waiters and waitresses are required. How do they manage to fight the traffic? Traffic lights, of course! Behind the Royal throne there are signals to direct servers to STOP, GET READY or GO. The penalty for running a light is not known.

An apple a day keeps the doctor away, so they say. Somehow King Otto of Bavaria got things a little mixed up. He was under the belief that killing a peasant a day would keep his doctors away. As a result the royal family and the king's doctors locked his 'royally insane' highness in his palatial bedroom, where he spent most of his time having spirited conferences with the ghosts he insisted were living in his dresser drawers.

After a week or so the King began to yell that he hadn't killed his peasant that day. The doctors decided to outsmart him. They had one of the palace guards dress up as a peasant and another give the King a gun loaded with blanks. From that day forth, from the window of the same room, at the same time each day, the King shot the same disguised guard with the same gun. He did it until the day he died!

# Odd laws

In Turkey in the 16th and 17th centuries, anyone caught drinking coffee was put to death. Perhaps this is the origin of caffeine being bad for your health?

## In 1659 Massachusetts lawmakers passed an ordinance outlawing Christmas.

In New York State it is illegal to shoot at a rabbit from a moving trolley car. Please get off the car, or wait for it to come to a complete stop, then fire away.

The Stiff But Warm Ordinance: during the late 17th century a law was passed in England requiring all corpses to be buried in a wool shroud. The intention was not to keep the bodies warm, but to drum up support for the national wool trade. The law was repealed 148 years later in 1814.

In Kansas there is a law which reads: 'When trains meet at a crossing, both shall come to a full stop and neither shall proceed until the other has gone.'

During the reign of Elizabeth I a law declared that any woman who led a man into marriage through the use of false hair, make-up, false hips, high heeled shoes or other devices, should be punished with the penalties of witchcraft.

Witchcraft was a serious crime in the Middle Ages. If a husband couldn't get a divorce, he could always accuse his wife of being a witch. Chances are the poor lady would be burned at the stake. Of course, they didn't simply take the husband's word for it. Being an enlightened society, or at least a society going through the Enlightenment, they had tests for that sort of thing: like trial by water. Court officials would tie the woman's feet and hands together and then drop her into some deep water. If she went straight to the bottom and drowned, it was a sure sign that she wasn't a witch and that the husband had made a mistake. On the other hand, if she didn't sink and just bobbed around for a while, the law said she was to be condemned as a witch. Divorce granted. In Holland skinny women had to be very careful – if they weighed in on the town scale light enough to ride a broomstick, they were burned to death.

In Minnesota residents may not put male and female underwear next to each other on the clothesline.

In Carmel, California, ice cream parlors were outlawed, until Clint Eastwood became mayor. The outlaw ice cream lover proclaimed that the town wasn't big enough for both of them. So the law went!

In Malaya it is against the law to dance on the backs of turtles.

In Cornwall, England, the penalty for defacing a bridge is still 'transportation to Australia'. Vandals, reach for your spray cans and surfboards...

## In Madagascar it is illegal for pregnant women to wear hats or eat eels.

A Nigerian witch doctor faces the death sentence if his bullet-proof charms fail to work.

## In Alaska it is illegal to look at a moose from the window of an airplane or any other flying vehicle.

In France, the process of naming a child is taken very seriously. French parents can face arrest for naming baby girls Prune, Cherry or Vanilla.

If a prisoner escapes from a certain jail in Alamos, Mexico, the guard on duty has to serve out the sentence. Needless to say, Alamos guards take their job *very* seriously.

Duelling is illegal in Uruguay – unless both parties are registered blood donors. In this case it is encouraged.

In the Malagasay Indian tribes it is against the law for a son to be taller than his father. If he is, it costs him either money or an ox.

# Odd laws

In Ottawa, Canada, there is a stinger of an anti-noise law which prohibits the buzzing of bees. No one is quite sure how the law should be enforced, since the bees seem to ignore the posted signs, they don't quite fit into the standard handcuffs and no police officers are willing to serve a warrant. Rumors buzzing around the local stations are that bees attack the long arm of the law whenever it reaches out for them.

**It is illegal to hunt camels in the state of Arizona.**

**In New York it is illegal to leave a naked dummy in a shop window overnight – they can be naked all day, but you have to dress them up at night.**

In Indiana it is against the law to travel on a bus within 4 hours of eating garlic. Rumor has it that the bill was initiated by a pale and quite obscure state legislator who came from Transylvania, Indiana.

During the reign of Elizabeth I the wearing of hats was made compulsory. According to the statute books: 'Every person above the age of 7 years shall wear upon the Sabbath and Holiday (unless in the time of their travels out of their towns, hamlets, etc) upon their head, a cap of wool knit, thicked and dressed in England, made within this Realm, and only dressed and finished by some of the Trade of Cappers, upon pain to forfeit for every day not wearing three shillings fourpence: except maids, ladies, gentlemen, noble personages, and every lord, knight and gentleman of 20 marks land and their heirs, and such as have borne Office of Worship in any City, Borough, Town, Hamlet or Shire; and the Wardens of the Worshipful Companies of London'. Hats off to anyone who understands that!

In Kenya there is a law which says that any foreigners caught running naked will be deported, naked, on the next plane out. The one advantage for the deportee is that he is not required to wait in line for the metal detector.

A taxi driver in Prague who turns the meter rate to level 3 (3 times faster than the legal rate of 1) is breaking the law UNLESS the ride is taking place following a nuclear explosion. Then, the sazba, or rate, of 3 is officially sanctioned by the Government.

In 1937 in Hungary spring cleaning became compulsory. All lofts, garrets and cellars had to be cleaned. Fines were imposed on citizens who did not comply.

In Idaho a citizen is forbidden by law to give another citizen a box of candy that weighs more than 50 lb.

In Venice in the 16th and 17th centuries prostitutes began wearing high heels because they felt they made them appear more attractive and, presumably, more marketable. The custom was taken to absurd lengths: women felt that the higher they went, the more a customer would pay for their services. Eventually city officials introduced a law banning high heels altogether – because women began to trip at night and fall to their deaths in the canals.

*Dogs didn't have to wear hats in Elizabethan England but everyone else did!*

**Every citizen of Kentucky is required by law to take a bath once a year.**

# Strange deaths

Spontaneous combustion – what a way to go! It's when a human body suddenly ignites and burns without any known external cause. The combustion of Mrs Mary Carpenter took place in front of her husband while they were on vacation on a cabin cruiser. She was sipping a drink in the lounge when suddenly she burst into flames. Over 200 similarly volatile cases have been reported in the last 400 years.

Recently, in Florida, Mrs Mary Reecer spontaneously combusted in her living-room. All that was left in the charred room was part of one leg, still wearing a shoe. The most sophisticated technology was used to investigate the phenomenon. The result: no logical explanation.

### Bela Lugosi, the most famous of all movie Draculas, died while reading a screenplay called *The Final Curtain*. He was buried wearing Dracula's cape.

Although sentenced to be hanged for murder, William Kogut swore he would kill himself rather than give the state the pleasure of executing him. Known in San Quentin as Convict Number 1651, Kogut was kept under constant surveillance to prevent any possibility of suicide.

He spent the bulk of his time playing solitaire. What his guards did not observe was that their ward was tearing out the red heart and diamond shapes from each card and storing them in a hollow leg in his bunk. On the night of October 9 1930, Kugot took the leg, filled it with water, sealed both ends, and placed it on a heater in his cell. Several hours later the make-shift pipe bomb, the cell and Kogut blew up.

What he knew, and his careless caretakers did not, was that the ink forming the red symbols contained nitrate and cellulose: an explosive mixture when combined with water. Kogut may have dealt his last card cheating the authorities, but he did not cheat death.

*All that remained of one victim of spontaneous human combustion.*

*The notorious Halifax Gibbett took boastful John Lacy's breath (and head) away.*

The Halifax Gibbet, a forerunner of the guillotine, has existed since 1286. For hundreds of years the law stated that if a condemned criminal could withdraw his head from the Gibbet between the time the blade was released and the time it hit the bottom, and could then run to the nearby town of Hebblebrook, he would be set free, unconditionally.

The only man successfully to challenge the Gibbet and run to freedom was John Lacy. For 7 years he boasted about his miraculous deed. People became tired of hearing about it and eventually stopped believing him.

So Lacy decided he must prove his story – and what better way than by doing it again?

He made his way back to Halifax, placed his neck in the Gibbet and smiled at the disbelievers as the blade was set free. You can probably guess the rest about 'Poor John Lacy'. As for the Halifax Gibbet, it was taken out of commission in 1650, but its ability to attract curious sightseers is still very much alive.

Convicted murderer Michael Godwin did not have to sit on the electric chair in Columbia, South Carolina. While he was on death row his sentence was commuted to life imprisonment.

Several weeks later he was trying to fix the electrical cord from the TV set in his new cell. For reasons known only to Godwin he bit into the cord – unfortunately while sitting on the metal frame of his bed. In a shocking twist of fate, he electrocuted himself by gnawing on the exposed wire.

# Strange deaths

The Marquis de Condorcet, a celebrated French mathematician and philospher, almost lost his head over an omelet. As a fugitive during the French Revolution, he entered an inn one day and asked for his favorite food – an omelet made with 12 eggs. His extravagant tastes made the innkeeper suspicious. He knew of no impoverished workman with a taste for such a dish. The innkeeper called the local guards, who immediately imprisoned the unfortunate Marquis with the intention of sending him to the guillotine. Next morning, however, the Marquis was found dead in his cell. Some thought he had been ill-treated, others believed he had poisoned himself. It was probably an overdose of cholesterol!

**A small stone marks the burial place, in Westminster Abbey, of the poet Ben Jonson. He was too poor to pay for the normal grave space, so he was buried standing up!**

At one time, when someone died friends and family were supposed not to eat a morsel of food, or drink anything but water, until after the funeral.

In order to save money on food for his family and servants, John Overs decided to play dead for a few days. To make the prank realistic, he enlisted the aid of his friend, a local doctor.

After the pronouncement of Overs' death, the 'body' was laid out on a table and covered with a sheet. As he lay pretending to be dead, he probably began calculating how much money he was saving that day. His family and servants, however, were so happy that the old skin-flint had died, they threw a party. They broke into the kitchen and ate everything they could lay their hands on. Apparently John heard the festivities going on and realized that his joke had backfired. Still under the sheet, he started to sit up and a terrified guest, thinking he was seeing a ghost, ran over to the fireplace, grabbed a log and gave the sheet-covered figure a mighty blow on the head. The party continued – but it was all over for John Overs!

Henry Trigg was a grocer by trade and a church warden by inclination. One night, after drinking at the Black Swan Inn in Hitchin, England, he decided to take a short cut through St Mary's Churchyard. Suddenly he found himself confronted by a pair of grave-robbers in the process of digging up a fresh corpse. After chasing off the robbers, Henry continued on his way. That night it dawned on him that he wouldn't be able to chase away those who might come to rob his grave so before he died in 1722 he came up with a lofty idea which he included in his will. He gave his brother his worldly wealth on condition that he build a loft in the rafters of the old barn behind his house. He instructed that his coffin be placed within it, instead of St Mary's Churchyard. After his death Henry's instructions were followed to the letter. When the coffin was opened by distant relatives in 1831, Henry was none the worse for wear. The coffin, and Henry, remained undisturbed for years. Then during World War I some Australian soldiers billeted in the barn discovered the coffin resting on the rafters. In it they found Henry's bones. What better memento of their stay in England to take back to Australia? The empty coffin can still be seen lying on the rafters of the barn in Hitchin. As for Henry Trigg, he avoided being dissected in a medical school only to end up as a souvenir in Australia.

To many people Gregory Rasputin was more than Czarina Alexandra's religious counselor and adviser. He was envisaged as the power behind the Romanov throne and a danger to the survival of the royal dynasty. Members of Czar Nicolas' court believed he possessed many supernatural powers. As his influence over the royal family increased it became more and more apparent that he had to be removed, by any means. A plan to murder him was conceived by members of the Czar's inner circle, including a Grand Duke, a Deputy, a doctor and a young Prince,

Felix Youssoupov. The murder was to be committed in the basement of the Youssoupov Palace.

On the pretence that there was a party at the Palace, Prince Youssoupov lured Rasputin into the basement, where a banquet had been prepared. Rasputin's royal host watched anxiously as his guest ate chocolates and cakes containing enough cyanide to kill several men. Astonishingly, Rasputin complimented the baker and chased the cake with several glasses of wine, also heavily laced with poison. The massive toxic doses had no effect on him. He simply kept eating and drinking, thoroughly enjoying the feast. To some of those present it merely served to confirm Rasputin's supernatural powers.

Finally Youssoupov, totally unnerved by the monk's indifference to his deadly meal, took a revolver and shot him at point blank range. Instantly Rasputin fell to the floor. The other conspirators entered the room and the doctor pronounced him dead. The group gathered in an anteroom to arrange for the disposal of the body. But Youssoupov had a sudden sinking feeling and returned to look at the

*Prince Felix Youssoupov, who killed Rasputin (left). Or did he?*

body. As he was bending over it, Rasputin grabbed the Prince by the neck and began to strangle him. Youssoupov managed to free himself and Rasputin, getting to his feet, staggered out to the courtyard. The Deputy, hearing the noise and seeing Rasputin attempting to escape, fired two shots, bringing him down yet again. For good measure he kicked him hard in the head. Youssoupov ran over and repeatedly struck Rasputin with a club. At last he was dead.

Taking no chances, the murderers tied the corpse's hands and feet and drove him to the river. There they threw the body from a bridge with such force that it cracked the thick covering of ice and sank from sight. Three days later the body was found. Rasputin's hands were free of their bonds, as though he had continued to struggle even under the ice.

The autopsy revealed that although he had been poisoned, shot 3 times and beaten repeatedly, Gregory Rasputin, the Mad Monk, had finally died by drowning!

# The natural world

More than half the world's fresh water is contained in the rivers and lakes of Canada. Where's the rest? A good deal of it lies in the Amazon River, which is so wide that one-fifth of the world's fresh water pours from its mouth. The Amazon is also the longest river in the world at 4,200 miles and drains an area of 2,772,000 miles.

*No water shortage here: the Amazon at its junction with the Rio Negro.*

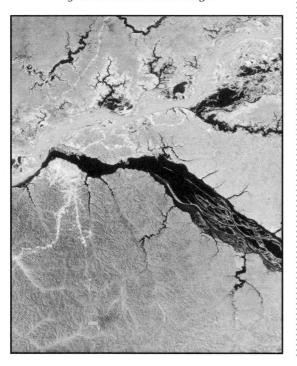

Lightning strikes the earth 100 times every second. There are 18,000 thunderstorms in progress at any given moment. Recently, scientists studying a single ridge near Castle Rock, Colorado, found that over a period of several years lightning struck the ridge more than 120,000 times. However, Central Florida apparently holds the world record for lightning strikes.

Experts claim that lightning is attracted to specific geographic points, especially where the sea hits coastal headlands. It is also inclined to take a fancy to tall, unexposed objects – such as a British Major called Summerford. You could say he was struck down in action during World War I.

He was struck by lightning not once, but 3 times. The last bolt killed him. In a shocking coincidence, 4 years later his tombstone was totally shattered – by lightning.

We have learned considerably more about lightning and electricity since Benjamin Franklin attracted it in 1752 with a key and a kite. One electrical pioneer, Michael Faraday, even put his life on the line to prove that with proper grounding, powerful charges of electricity will circumvent large bodies of metal. To test his theory, the daring Faraday built himself a metal cage, got inside and had his assistant generate a massive charge

**A single drop of water contains some 1.7 quintillion – 1,700,000,000,000,000,000 molecules.**

**If that single drop of water were to be perfectly diluted by all the water in all the oceans and lakes in the world, every pint of the resulting dilution would contain about 24 of the original drop's molecules.**

of electricity through it. Fortunately, the charge acted exactly as he had predicted. Instead of going right through the cage, and him, it went around it. Because of Faraday's electrifying experiment, we now know we're safe when lightning strikes an airplane or an automobile.

Alaska is neither here nor there. Why, or how, you ask? Well, it is the northern-most, western-most and, amazingly, the eastern-most state in the United States. It extends so far west it crosses the Eastern Hemisphere line. You could get lost in Alaska even when you know exactly where you are.

Hold on to your hats, and anything else which is not nailed down, the next time you pay a visit to Commonwealth Bay, George V Coast, Antarctica. It is the windiest place in the world, with gales reaching as much as 200 mph.

It turns out that the average hurricane might not be so average. If it could be harnessed, the energy could supply the electrical power used by every household in the US for half a year. The amount of energy would be equivalent to exploding 10 atomic bombs every second for the whole of those 6 months!

*Getting the wind up in a big way. Pity the power behind this Texan tempest could not be harnessed for human use.*

## IT'S A FACT

A particularly ferocious hurricane on March 15-16 1952 unloaded a record 73.62 in of rain in a mere 24 hours in Cilaos, near the Indian Ocean. This is equal to 8,327 tons of rain per acre.

**If the number of humans on planet earth were to continue to increase at the current rate, by 3530 AD the total weight of all the living human bodies would equal the mass of the earth itself. That's the best argument yet for space exploration. Given the same rate of population expansion, by the year 6826 AD the total mass of humanity will equal the size of the entire known universe.**

Hundreds of years ago man knew enough to postulate that if he could harness the energy of the sun, his energy problems would be solved for ever. We now know that he was right: the earth receives a mere one half of one billionth of the sun's light and heat energy, but in just 3 days this amounts to as much heat and light as could be produced by burning all the coal, oil and wood on the planet at the same time.

Fire is usually considered to be a destructive force, but for the giant sequoia trees of California it is vital to survival. Whereas most trees distribute their seeds as soon as they mature, the sequoia retains them in cones, sometimes for decades. When a natural fire occurs, hot updrafts dry and open the cones, thereby releasing seeds which shower on to the forest floor. The freshly burned floor, cleared by the fire of undergrowth and competing trees, provides the sequoia seedlings with access to sunlight and soil minerals, thus perpetuating the species. If natural fires don't happen periodically, the US Forest Service has to create them to ensure the continuity of the trees.

Throughout the universe planets and stars are gaining and shedding weight every day. In fact, as a result of space dust and meteorites in particular, the earth increases its weight by almost 20 tons per day. The sun, on the other hand, is losing weight. Each day nearly 360 million tons of gas and solid material are released during explosions on the sun's surface. But, since a million earths could fit into the sun, scientists don't expect this galactic weight problem to have any effect on our solar system's balance of power.

*A massive solar flare. Explosions on the sun's surface are a daily occurrence.*

When Tambura, the Philippines volcano, erupted in 1815 it created a dust cloud that blanketed over half of the earth's sky for more than a year. Between 50 and 100 cubic miles of soil, minerals and soot exploded into the air: the equivalent of removing 2 ft from the entire surface of Texas.

The dust cloud resulted in the years known to New Englanders as 'eighteen hundred and froze to death' (1816). It snowed in June, frost killed crops in July, August and September, throughout the summer shorn sheep froze to death and migrating birds were thrown off course.

Between spring 1816 and spring 1817 the world seemed locked in a perpetual winter as the Arctic Cap grew, glaciers advanced and the sea level dropped. Those 12 months of winter were colder than any since.

In Batticaloa, Sri Lanka, there is a singing lake. On calm nights, especially at full moon, musical notes can clearly be heard. The sounds appear to come from the bottom of the lake, and if a long pole is thrust into the water and the upper end placed against the ear, the singing can be heard loudly. Experts believe the sound is caused by a kind of shellfish which inhabits the lake. What the experts can't explain is why these creatures like to sing.

On the island of Gozo, off Malta, there is a rare plant called *Fungus Gaulanus*, believed by the Knights of St John to possess strong healing powers. This rare plant was, for centuries, kept under constant guard. The penalty for stealing the fungus was instant death.

The banana tree isn't a tree at all. Actually, it's a giant herb – the largest plant on earth without a woody stem. A banana plant will bear fruit only once, but each rootstock of the plant can, in turn, produce an unending series of plants. Each plant bears an average 150 bananas, more than 90 lb of fruit.

*It sounds bananas, but this banana tree isn't a tree at all - it's a herb.*

# Animal tales

**A newly-hatched crocodile is 3 times as large as the actual egg from which it emerges.**

When exposed to oxygen, mammals' blood is red and insects' blood is bright yellow. In the animal kingdom only lobsters are truly worthy of being referred to as 'blue bloods'.

At birth most mammals weigh about 1/20th of the weight of their mother; this is the case with human beings and most monkeys. But the bear cub at birth is smaller in proportion to the size of the mother than any other mammal except marsupials. A new-born cub is only 8-10 in long and weighs some 12 to 15 oz. Adult female bears weigh in the region of 500 lb or more, so the average cub is a mere 1/500th of its mother's weight at birth.

There is a fish in the Antarctic which has white blood: it is the only fish known to have no red pigment in its blood stream. Normally, the lack of haemoglobin means an end to the fun, since oxygen cannot be delivered to the cells without it. But the white-blooded fish seems to enjoy good health regardless.

The average jelly fish is over 90 per cent water, yet it can be one of the deadliest beasts in the ocean. The lethal ingredient is in the other 10 per cent. Since some jellyfish can grow to nearly 100 ft across, that 10 per cent can pack a lot of wallop.

*A watery customer to steer clear of: the Portuguese Man-o'War.*

Can chocolate-covered ants be considered brain food? Possibly. In proportion to its size, the common ant has the largest brain of any other creature on earth.

## The European oyster that lives off the coast of Denmark changes its sex from male to female and back again every 5 years. And all this without an operation.

The Roman Emperor, Caligula, appointed his favorite horse Incitatus as consul and co-regent of Rome. Caligula always invited his horse to dine with him, but his successor, Claudius, decided this was a little too much. He did, however, ensure that the horse was well looked after, even providing him with a golden goblet for his wine.

Blackbird, a Chief of the Omaha Indian tribe, spent most of his waking hours on his horses, usually in battle. His last mount was his favorite, so Blackbird gave instructions that when he died he was to be buried sitting on his beloved companion. Unfortunately for the horse, Blackbird died first – the animal which had survived Blackbird's fiercest battles didn't survive his master's funeral.

---

**IT'S A FACT**

The Chihuahua is the smallest dog on earth, weighing in at between 2 and 4 lb. Some specimens have tipped the scales at a mere 16 oz.

The largest land animal in all of Antarctica is the wingless fly. Presumably if it had wings, it would fly to a more hospitable climate.

# Animal tales

**There are millions of different species and subspecies of mammals, insects, reptiles, fish and birds alive today, but 99 per cent of all forms of life that have ever existed on earth is now extinct.**

Measuring up to 110 ft in length and weighing some 200 tons – the equivalent of 2,000 people – the blue whale is the largest animal in the world today. It is also the largest animal which has ever lived on earth, nearly twice the size of the largest dinosaur. It emits the loudest sound produced by a living creature: its whistle, at 188 decibels, is more deafening than the roar of a passing jet aircraft.

The sperm whale has the largest brain of any animal. Weighing in at around 20 lb, it is 6 times the size of the average human brain. The sperm whale also has highly sophisticated sensory and sonar capacities, enabling it to hunt for squid and other life forms in total darkness at depths of more than 5,000 ft.

The humpback whale's underwater songs can be heard hundreds of miles away. Thanks to sensitive listening devices on NASA's *Voyager*, the humpback's tune is known to carry into the far reaches of the solar system – and beyond.

The Bowhead whale's mouth is roomy enough to accommodate 2 mid-size pick-up trucks parked side by side. Now that's what you call Max-Headroom!

The gray whale has the longest migration pattern of any mammal: 7,000 miles, from the Arctic to the waters off Mexico.

**If you think you have a weight problem, consider the young blue whale who can gain more than 300 lb – a day!**

Las Vegas, Nevada, is the home to more neon, more slot machines and more gambling tables than any other city in the world. It is also home to the Mirage Hotel, which has a specially constructed pool for an endangered species – dolphins. Why are dolphins on the way out? To begin with, they are slaughtered by the thousands on a daily basis when they get caught in tuna-fishing nets. Also, as mammals, they breathe oxygen, which we humans are managing to destroy with fossil-fuel pollution and a disregard for the preservation of the ozone layer.

At the Mirage, the dolphins are able to breathe clean desert air. How ironic that a creature of the sea stands the best chances of survival 500 miles inland in the middle of the desert.

**The average tuna swims at a steady speed of 9 mph and, since they don't sleep, they never stop moving. This means that a 15-year-old tuna will have traveled one million miles in its lifetime, which works out at being the equivalent of swimming around the world nearly 40 times.**

Migrating ducks fly for thousands of miles at speeds of up to 60 mph; racing pigeons can zip around at 100 mph; peregrine falcons have been timed at 217 mph and the spine-tailed swift has been clocked at an astonishing 220 mph. Swift in flight, indeed!

The most outstanding flight recorded for any homing pigeon during World War II was made by a bird named G.I. Joe. On the morning of October 18 1943 the British had gained a victory over German forces in a small village in Italy. It was necessary to call off the air cover that had been requested by the Allied forces. All communication lines were down and G.I Joe carried the message in time to prevent the support planes from taking off.

His flight saved the lives of more than 1,000 British soldiers. He was given a medal by the Lord Mayor of London and special recognition by the Congress of the United States.

*Pigeon-power helped win World War II!*

An ostrich's brain weighs less than one of its eyeballs. Quite often ostriches can spot a predator approaching at high speed. Their problem is that they can't always think fast enough to get out of its way.

# Animal tales

*Would you pay $3,500
for this masterpiece by Ruby?*

A few years ago Ruby the elephant, who lives in the Phoenix Zoo, used to pass the time tempting ducks from a nearby pond with pieces of food, drawing them within striking range, and then crushing them with her foot.

The zoo-keepers, distressed by Ruby's behavior, realized that it was caused by boredom. Struck by a peculiar habit of hers – she picked up sticks with her trunk and seemed to draw in the dirt, sometimes for hours – they decided to indulge her habit in an attempt to keep her happy. Gradually Ruby's interest in drawing seemed to increase, so her keepers supplied her with paint, brushes and sheets of cardboard and she began to paint. Eventually they provided her with her own custom-built easel.

Ruby is now a celebrated artist, with an 'office' at the zoo. The keepers, who assist her by holding brushes and palettes for her choosing, have found that she prefers primary colors, and often paints the colors and objects she encounters throughout the day. She is the source of much discussion among scientists, who had previously believed elephants to be color blind. Today Ruby is a mammoth attraction at the zoo and earns as much as $3,500 for one of her works. The zoo-keepers, and the ducks, couldn't be happier with her new found talent.

An elephant uses its trunk for a variety of functions – from defending itself against predators to bathing its offspring. This extended nose-like appendage is truly an all-purpose limb. Well, almost. In order to smell, the elephant uses its mouth.

Elephants can weigh as much as 4 tons, yet they walk on their tip-toes, distributing their weight with the efficiency of a ballerina. Physicists insist that while elephants may be the heaviest and most voluminous creatures on land, the average elephant puts less pressure on the ground in any one spot than the average woman wearing high heels.

Most fish are insomniacs, being constantly in motion, with only occasional periods of slower movement. Some rare fish in the coral reefs do drift off to sleep for periods of time. They stand on their tails.

The blood pressure of the giraffe is 3 times that of a healthy human – the highest in the world. Why? To get the blood all the way up that 10-12 ft neck. The giraffe's heart is enormous, too: on average it weighs 25 lb, is 2 ft long and has walls up to 3 in thick.

Giraffes are afraid of heights. In fact, they will step down no more than 18 in. Their fear is possibly due to their lack of depth perception, stemming from their lofty perspective on the world. Yet, even though a giraffe's head can rise as much as 10 ft above its torso, it has the same number of vertebrae as the average human.

Some kangaroos can bound more than 30 ft with each jump. One large kangaroo has been measured clearing a woodpile 10.5 ft high and 27 ft long, comparable to vaulting over a bus.

The orang-utan, the black lion tamarin and the Celebes black ape may be on their way to extinction. Why? Because of human taste for tropical hardwood furniture. For every such dining-room chair or table, another tree disappears from the rain-forests, the natural habitat of the orang-utan and the Celebes black ape.

The same could be said for the South American spectacled Bear, named for its unique facial markings. Human hunting activities in the Andes Mountains of Chile, Columbia, Ecuador, Bolivia and Peru have sadly brought the spectacled bear to the verge of extinction.

At Croaker College in Emeryville, California, students have access to whirlpool baths, hypnosis, physical education and gourmet meals, and are taught a variety of tricks. All quite run-of-the mill for the average Californian college, except that all the students are frogs.

**Don't try to hurt a hippopotamus' feelings: the skin of the average hippo is over 2 in thick!**

# Animal tales

To the Earl of Bridgewater, the dog was truly man's best friend. One thing's for sure, the Earl was certainly his dog's best friend. Every night he personally prepared a formal dinner – tables set with crystal and fine china, gourmet foods, fine wines and servants – specially for his dogs. Were he alive today, the Earl wouldn't have to go to quite so much trouble. He could simply have his canine friends accompany him for dinner at Maxim's in Paris. There they have a separate, and very elegant, menu for canine companions.

Being treated like a dog could be no bad thing. Imagine life in one of the canine mansions designed by architect Mette Farmer. The top of the range Palladian Palace has stone dog statues adorning the turrets, raised sleeping quarters, bean bags, cushions and a sophisticated ventilation system. For the design-conscious dog, a mural can be included. Although Ms Farmer has a set of basic designs, each kennel is tailor-made for its occupant. Being in the doghouse suddenly seems quite desirable!

**IT'S A FACT**

**It is illegal to own a dog in Reykjavik, Iceland.**

Following the death of a shepherd from Fort Benton, Montana, his family arranged for the body to be transported to burial in another city. The shepherd's faithful dog watched from the station as the body was loaded onto a train. Thereafter, the dog patiently waited for his master to return. He waited 6 years. The townspeople and the Station Master made him as comfortable as possible, but they could not persuade him to leave the station. Finally, on January 12 1942, Shep was killed by one of the trains he had run to meet. He was buried with full ceremony, and a monument was erected over the grave: a profile statue of Shep, which can be seen clearly from passing trains.

Marco, a Belgian shepherd, is the world's most wanted dog. Mexican drug traffickers have issued posters offering a reward of $25,000 for Marco, dead or alive. The reason? He is a champion sniffer. He has detected over 10 tonnes of marijuana, 500 kg of cocaine and 8 kg of heroin. But catching Marco el Narco, as he is known, will prove very difficult. He sleeps with his trainer and only eats imported American dog food – for security reasons.

In 1888 Ooney, a mongrel of uncertain age, appeared in the Albany, New York, where he was befriended by postal workers. Ooney had an affinity with mail pouches, and liked particularly to sleep on leather. One day he rode a pouch on the carriage to the train station and hopped on to the train along with the pouch for what was to be his first journey – to New York City. The Albany post office put a tag on him bearing the inscription 'post office, Albany, New York'.

Ooney quickly became a seasoned traveler, though he always returned to Albany. Once, the people at the post office there raised money to liberate him from the pound of a small city in Canada.

They asked postal workers in other cities to fit him with a metal tag identifying where he had been. In time, there were so many tags that Ooney's collar had to be replaced with a harness. He just kept traveling, so the harness was quickly covered, too. From time to time friendly postal workers would remove some of the tags and send them to Albany.

In 1897 Ooney clearly felt he had seen everything there was to see in the United States, so he embarked on a round-the-world trip from Takoma, Washington, on a mail steamship. He went to Yokohama, Shanghai, Singapore and Algiers, returning via New York City and then across country to Takoma. He was given dozens of medals by various kennel clubs for being the most traveled mongrel.

In 1897 he took his last trip west, to San Francisco. He attended the National Association of Railway Postal Clerks meeting. There he received a 15-minute ovation. When he finally came to rest on June 11 1897, he had traveled more than 143,000 miles.

I n November 1992 a British astronaut was strapped into the Soyuz rocket capsule with gifts from the Russian people and a message from President Boris Yeltsin. The rocket orbited the world before splashing down off Seattle, where it was recovered by the Russian warship *Marshal Krilov*. The captain of the *Krilov* personally delivered the new British celebrity to Seattle. His name is Digswell, and at 2ft tall, Digswell the Dog, the mascot of American's Young Astronauts Council, became the first stuffed British astronaut to be made a freeman of the city of Seattle (or of any city for that matter).

*Ben the pampered pig expects - and receives - all the attention any hog could hope for.*

S ome pigs have all the luck. While his brothers around the world are confined in muddy pens, forced to eat grain, Ben lives in Hog Heaven. Ben was adopted by Maria Hennesey at the Sanctuary for Injured Animals in Gwent, Wales, provided a brick-built home, complete with a chimney, for Santa Claus, and windows with lace curtains. The house is called 'Pigmalion'. Over the years Ben's reputation has spread. He has a fan club and receives letters from all over the world, which Maria answers on Ben's own letterhead. Basking in fame, Ben, a vegetarian, wakes late, lounges around, and then prepares for his meals – which often include his favorite drink: strawberry milkshake.

**IT'S A FACT**

**Black Boy of Black Mountain, North Carolina, was the most portly pig in recorded history. In 1939 he crushed the scales at 1,904 lb.**

# Animal tales

*Is it a bat? Is it a rat?
Or is it that the inhabitants of Bavaria have
had one too many?*

Wolperdingers are purported to be the ugliest and most bizarre creatures on the face of the planet. For centuries drunks and the mentally deranged have reported seeing them in the forests of Bavaria. Today the locals have developed a tradition of frolicking in the woods at night in an attempt to bag one. Few know what they will do with the ugly creature if they find it and since it's night, and most of the participants are drunk to begin with, it's little wonder that no one has yet caught a Wolperdinger.

A Miami federal agent in a gorilla outfit helped catch Mexican zoo officials suspected of smuggling primates into Mexico. Authorities said the agent was in a cage while Victor Bernal, zoos and parks director for the interior state of Mexico, was arranging a $92,500 deal.

The skeletal mass of some mammals can account for as much as one-third of their total body weight. But the pigeon's feathers alone weigh more than its bones.

In England and Continental Europe during the Middle Ages it was illegal for any animal to injure or kill a human being. It was even common practice to try and condemn animals for offenses. In one documented case, the French parliament, the highest court in the nation, ordered the execution of a cow. It was hanged and then burned at the stake.

## There are 450 million chickens in the United States - twice as many chickens as people. So much for majority rule!

At Hang-zhou in eastern China 140 chickens were fitted with rose-tinted contact lenses. The idea was to calm the chickens and increase egg production. Do the birds have to take the lenses out at night and put them in soaking solution?

---

**In Elizabethan times it became popular to refer to groups of animals by names that seemed to suit species, for example, a 'pride' of lions or a 'gaggle' of geese. Here are some more:**

| | | |
|---|---|---|
| a bale of turtles | a drove of cattle or sheep | a pod of whales or seals |
| a band of gorillas | a gam of whales | a school of fish |
| a bed of clams or oysters | a gang of elks | a sedge or siege of cranes |
| a bevy of quail or swans | a grist of bees | a shoal of pilchards or fish |
| a brace of ducks | a herd of elephants | a skein of geese |
| a brood of chicks | a horde of gnats | a skulk of foxes |
| a cast of hawks | a husk of hares | a sleuth of bears |
| a cete of badgers | a kindle or kendle of kittens | a sounder of boars or swine |
| a charm of goldfinches | a knot of toads | a span of mules |
| a clout of gnats | a leap of leopards | a spring of teals |
| a clowder of cats | a leash of greyhounds/foxes | a swarm of bees |
| a clutch of chicks | a litter of pigs | a team of horses or ducks |
| a clutter of cats | a mob of kangaroos | a tribe or trip of goats |
| a colony of ants | a murder of crows | a troop of kangaroos or monkeys |
| a congregation of plover | a muster of peacocks | a volery of birds |
| a covey of quail or partridge | a mute of hounds | a watch of nightingales |
| a crash of rhinoceri | a nest of vipers | a wing of plovers |
| a cry of hounds | a nest or nide of pheasants | a yoke of oxen |
| a down of hares | a pack of hounds or wolves | |
| a drift of swine | a pair of horses | |

# Remarkable people

When physician Sir James Barry died at the age of 73 his valet made an astounding discovery: Sir James was a woman! Barry was the first female physician in the British military, becoming the first female surgeon general. At a time when the medical profession was barred to women, Barry kept her secret for 57 years spent in the Army. She was never seen naked, rarely if ever socialized and never married.

*Sir James Barry.*
*He was actually a she!*

Thomas Parr was born in the Parish of Alberbury in Shropshire, England in 1483 during the reign of Edward V. He worked as a farmer during the reigns of Richard III, Henry VII, Henry VIII, Edward IV and Queen Mary. When Queen Elizabeth came to the throne, Thomas Parr was 75 and still farming.

He married for the first time in 1563 at the age of 80. In time James I succeeded Elizabeth but it made no difference to Parr – he just kept farming. He outlived his first wife, married again at the age of 122 and outlived this wife, too, as well as his children and grandchildren by his first wife.

In 1635, when Parr was 152, Charles I heard of his astounding longevity and invited him to London for a royal feast. Before dinner, the King asked Parr the secret of long life. 'Simple meals of grains and meats,' was the reply. 'Marvelous,' said the King as he offered Parr goose livers and baby eels basted in butter and onions, followed by fried sheep's eyeballs. Throughout the banquet, Parr regaled the King with stories while the King saw to it that Parr's plate and glass were always full. Unfortunately Parr, overwhelmed by the food, expired during the meal.

The distraught King, feeling responsible, had him buried in Westminster Abbey among the royal and noble dead of England. The inscription states that 'he lived 152 years, through the reigns of 10 Monarches'.

**What it doesn't say is that he died from eating food fit for a king!!**

John Merrick was one of the most extraordinary human beings who ever lived. He suffered from a rare bone disease which deformed him grotesquely: his right arm was like a giant claw, his right leg was nearly twice normal size. His head was enlarged and misshapen, his scaly skin reeked of a peculiar odor. When young he had a 9 in growth protruding from his mouth, which gave rise to the nickname 'The Elephant Man'. Although the growth was removed when he was 14, the unfortunate name stayed with him.

Merrick made a reasonable living as a freak in Tom Norman's peep show. It was there that he was seen by the eminent surgeon, Frederick Treeves. Merrick's painful deformities disturbed and fascinated Treeves. He took him into his private care, set up an apartment for him in the London Hospital and give him a mask to wear while walking the halls so as not to frighten the other patients and staff.

Treeves soon discovered that 'The Elephant Man' had considerable intelligence and spoke like a poet. Treeves' friends began to visit Merrick, initially to look, but in time to talk. Merrick never complained of his pain and suffering, but always kept his, and other's, spirits high. His reputation spread. Members of the Royal Family, particularly Princess Alexandra, were among those who repeatedly visited him.

The beauty of his soul had escaped the prison of his body, but his illness continued to progress. As he became

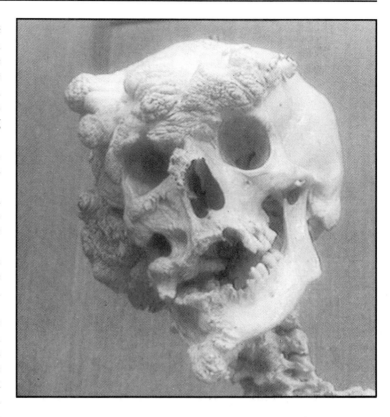

*The preserved remains of John Merrick, otherwise known as 'The Elephant Man'.*

weaker, walking became an exhausting process, and he was forced to spend more and more time in bed. Because of the huge weight of his head, he could only sleep sitting up. One night, at the age of 27, Merrick laid his head down and died. Among the few things he left behind were these lines of verse, written shortly before his death:

'Was I so tall I could reach the pole
or grasp the ocean with a span
I would be measured by the soul
the mind's the measure of the man.'

Merrick's skeleton, preserved in the London Hospital, is proof of the terrible disease from which he suffered. It also gives testimony to the dignity of man.

# Remarkable people

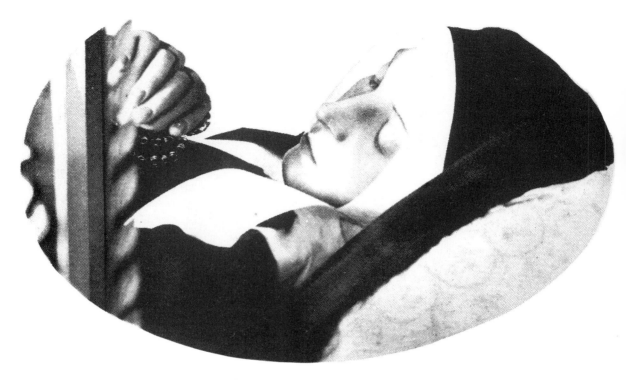

*St Bernadette pictured on her deathbed in 1879. More than a century later she still looks as beautiful as the day she died.*

It has been said that the prospect of timeless beauty lessens with the passage of time. But consider the case of Bernadette Soubirous, a peasant girl whose appearance seems as if it has remained unchanged since she died in 1879.

Born in Lourdes in France, in 1844, Bernadette was 14 when she saw a vision of the Virgin Mary, who told her of the miraculous healing powers of the underground spring near a grotto by her home. Bernadette told the local priest. He told the Bishop. The Bishop told everyone else. Eventually the grotto at Lourdes became a place of pilgrimage. Bernadette didn't believe in the spring's ability to heal and soon left Lourdes to become a nun in the convent of St Gildard in Nevers.

For a number of years she aided the sick and unfortunate but at the age of 35 she died. She was buried in the convent grounds, where a replica of the Grotto at Lourdes was erected. Thirty years later, in 1909, word came from Rome that Bernadette was eligible for sainthood. Accordingly, her body was exhumed. In spite of the fact that she hadn't been embalmed it was found to be in perfect condition. During the next 25 years she was exhumed twice more – and each time there was no change.

Finally the Holy Fathers were convinced that this peasant girl from Lourdes truly was a saint. She was canonized in 1933 and rests in the Chapel at St Gildard, in a crystal coffin, still looking exactly as she did the day she died.

Arthur Ferguson was known by public and police alike as The Con Man. In 1923 Ferguson, a Scot, set out to seek his fortune. Wandering the streets of London, he got into conversation with a man from Iowa, who was gazing lovingly at the statue of Nelson in Trafalgar Square.

The man explained that Lord Nelson was his hero – and Ferguson realized that he had just found himself a career. He introduced himself as a representative of the British Government and confided sadly that, in order to settle huge debts, the Government had to sell Nelson's Column for the knock-down price of $30,000.

The only condition was that the purchaser must have a deep respect and love for England's history. The man from Iowa was delighted to find that he would be considered suitable, and promptly arranged for the money to be wired to London, where he handed it over to Ferguson.

The wily Scot subsequently sold Big Ben for £1,000 (delivery proved to be something of a problem) and accepted a deposit of £2,000 for Buckingham Palace – both from gullible American tourists. Moving to the source of this new income, he sold the Statue of Liberty to an Australian businessman. However, before he handed over the $100,000 the Australian asked to have a picture of himself with Ferguson. So much for Ferguson. He spent 5 years in jail for fraud. He died in 1938 after spending his last years in comfort from the small fortune he had saved from his short but lucrative career.

John Patee built the Patee Hotel in St Joseph, Missouri, in the 1850s. An honest, hardworking man, he was moderate in his habits and never gambled. Well, almost never: just twice.

When the Civil War broke out, Patee judged that the south would emerge the victor. So that's who he backed. When the Confederacy was defeated, so was Patee. He lost his fortune.

But Patee was a resourceful man. With the little cash he managed to scrape together, he took another gamble. He printed 100,000 lottery tickets and hawked them from coast to coast for $2.00 each. The prize to the winner was his hotel. He sold all the tickets except 100, which he bought himself. And that's when fate stepped in. The winning ticket number was 50813: it belonged to John Patee.

Because of his reputation as an honest man, and the trusting nature of the citizens of St Joseph, no one questioned the result. Patee kept his hotel, over $100,000 in cash, and lived happily ever after.

Johann Sebastian Bach was not the only member of the Bach family to have musical talent. His great grandfather, Hans Bach, was known as 'the playing man', and two of Hans' grandsons, Johann Michael and Johann Sebastian achieved fame as musicians.

During the 17th century the musicians of the Bach family were so numerous and so distinguished that the name Bach became synonymous with music. Johann Sebastian, who was taught music by his father and elder brother, was married twice, both times to singers, and had 20 children, 5 of whom grew up to be eminent musicians. Carl Philipp Emanuel was the most distinguished.

In all, the Bach family produced almost 50 musicians.

Johann Sebastian's eldest son, Wilhelm Friedemann or 'Halle' Bach, was a brilliant organ player. He wrote numerous compositions, like his father, but few survive because he couldn't be bothered to write them down!

# Remarkable people

Britain's Lord Uxbridge, who helped defeat Napoleon at Waterloo, was sitting astride his horse, next to the Duke of Wellington, when he was shot in the leg. 'By God, Sir, I've lost my leg,' Uxbridge exclaimed. Wellington looked away from the battle just long enough to reply, 'By God, Sir, so you have!'

Uxbridge was taken, along with the severed leg, to the home of a local forester named Hyacinth Perres. There the wound was dressed and the seemingly worthless limb thrown out the window into the garden, where it was buried. The one-legged Uxbridge returned to England and a hero's welcome. A monument was erected in his honor and the war hero became a national figure.

Some time later, British tourists knocked on the forester's door asking to see where Uxbridge's leg had been buried. They were willing to pay to see it so Hyacinth, realizing there was money to be made, dug up the decaying leg, clothed it

*Who would believe a Lord's leg deserved its own funeral!*

and placed it on display. The leg was eventually given a funeral, attended by Uxbridge, with full military honors.

Uxbridge, who had returned from war to lead the genteel life of an aristocrat (he was ultimately Earl of Anglesey) got about with the help of an artificial leg – the world's first articulated prosthesis. When he died at the age of 86 most of him was buried in the family vault in Lichfield Cathedral, Wales, the rest of him being 500 miles away near Waterloo.

Uxbridge is probably the first person to have attended his own funeral twice – once as a guest and once as a participant. Like his first severed limb, the Earl's artificial leg was not buried with him either!

Anthony Shiels, widely known as Doc Shiels, is based in Cornwall, England, and is an all-round wizard, author, poet, playwright and artist! In 1977, he initiated the Monstermind project, organizing psychics and magicians to raise up lake monsters around the world. He photographed the Loch Ness Monster and Morgawr, the monster of Falmouth Bay, Cornwall. His other pursuits include the Little People, the winged owlman of Cornwall, giant squids, sky-clad witches, UFOs and the Irish Pooka.

Will Purvis, accused of murdering a Mississippi farmer, protested his innocence but was sentenced to be hanged. After the jury had found him guilty, Purvis proclaimed, 'I'll live to see every last one of you die!'

The date for the hanging was set and the gallows built. The noose was placed around Purvis' neck. The trap doors flung open and Purvis plunged to purgatory – or so everyone thought. The noose, however, had became loose and slipped over Purvis' neck. He had fallen to the ground with a crash. The sheriff was willing to give it another try, but the spectators thought that it was a miracle and that Purvis should be set free.

Not wishing to lose his own neck, the sheriff took Purvis back to his cell. Before a new date could be set for the execution Purvis' friends smuggled him out of jail and into hiding.

Thousands of letters asking for clemency poured into the Governor's office and Purvis was eventually pardoned. Many years later a dying man confessed to the murder for which Will Purvis had been condemned.

Will Purvis died on October 13 1938, 3 days after the death of the last juror who had sentenced him to hang. He had indeed seen every last one of them die.

Joseph-Edouard Beaupré was born on January 9 1881. At the age of 7, he suddenly began to grow . . and grow . . . until, at 17, he measured 8 ft 3 in. He had a 24-in neck, a 58-in chest, a 52-in waist and wore size 24 shoes. As an adult he weighed 396 lb. He became known as the Willow Bunch Giant, after his home town in Saskatchewan, Canada.

When fully grown he traveled across Canada exhibiting his size and strength in side-shows, eventually joining the Barnum Brothers Circus. In 1904, at the age of 23, he died suddenly in St Louis, Missouri.

His family could not afford to have his body returned to Willow Bunch so the circus obtained permission from local authorities to embalm it and exhibit it in a coffin.

Eventually, the embalmer took possession of the body and continued to exhibit it until the police intervened. It was taken to Montreal and placed in the Eden Museum, until that, too, closed.

Abandoned, the body of the Willow Bunch Giant was lost.

It was rediscovered in 1907 by children playing in a shed and given to the University of Montreal, where it remained until 1989. Ovila Lespérance, a nephew of the Willow Bunch Giant, had been trying since 1975 to obtain his uncle's body for burial. Eventually, the remains were cremated and his ashes buried on July 7 1990 – 86 years after his death.

**Fons Oelermans specializes in crossing the Atlantic Ocean by unconventional means. He has accomplished this feat in, among other things, a hot water cylinder, and a Dodge truck (the 3,000-mile 'drive' took 52 days). For his latest attempt he plans to utilize a 12-meter long diesel-powered bottle.**

Giuseppe Demai of Naples was born with two hearts. It was a phenomenon so bizarre that the London Academy of Medicine offered Giuseppe $15,000 if he would donate his body to science upon his death. Giuseppe Demai is the only man who could leave his heart in San Francisco...twice!

When Louis François Roubillac began his sculpture of composer George Frederick Handel he decided that Handel's ears were rather unsightly. So although the sculpture he created resembled Handel in every other way, the ears were modeled on the more attractive ears of a London lady. The statue can be seen in Westminster Abbey, London.

# Strange occupations

In the perfume industry, people are employed to smell. Referred to as 'noses', they have to distinguish 19,000 different odors at 20 levels of intensity.

Robert Connolly, a geneticist at Liverpool University, performs detailed studies of mummies to locate their former relatives. Essentially, he makes family trees for mummies by following their bloodlines. He does this by establishing blood groups. This would seem to be a difficult task since mummies do not have blood, but for Connolly it does not present a problem. He simply pulverizes a sliver of the mummy's tissue and mixes it with type-O blood, which then, remarkably, takes on the characteristics of the mummy's blood,

*To geneticist Robert Connolly locating a mummy's relatives is child's play.*

revealing its DNA sequence: its genetic fingerprints. By matching these 'prints' with those of other mummies he determines how they are related to each other. 3,500 years after death, Robert Connolly is able to bring mummy's blood back to life in order to determine the mummy's daddy – or mummy!

The Office of Currency Standards (OCS) in the Bureau of Printing and Engraving is in charge of, among other things, maintaining a current quality standard in the US money supply. They have worked on bills which have been shot from guns, scrubbed in washing machines, chopped in cocktail blenders and even poached in a water bed. One of the most complicated jobs the Currency Examiners had to deal with was when an armored car exploded. These dedicated individuals managed to reconstitute $2.5 million worth of notes from the remnants of the explosion.

Perhaps one of their most bizarre assignments was when a farmer killed a cow that had eaten his wallet and sent its stomach, containing the dollar bills, to the OCS in Washington DC. There the Currency Examiners managed to piece together $473 of the $600 that was in the wallet. The balance was the price the farmer paid for a dinner.

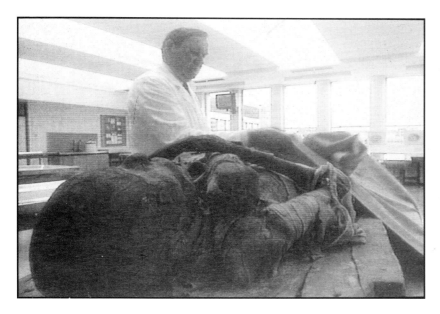

Two weeks of training at UCLA in California qualifies students to become Water Sniffers. Their job is to test samples of water in the Los Angeles basin. Salty, sour, bitter, earthy, fishy and septic scents indicate that something is amiss in the reservoirs. But, don't think that this job requires merely a nose ... it takes expertise and a knack of being able to handle the most fetid of aromas. Just like fine wine tasters, water sniffers hold the bottom of the glass so as not to affect the temperature of the liquid. They even nibble on unsalted crackers between sniffs and tastings. They have yet to declare a vintage year, but in Los Angeles anything is possible.

It is not unusual to see researchers at Cornell University dressing in strange leather hats with feathers and performing a bizarre, ritualistic mating dance. The idea is to encourage peregrine falcons to swoop down from the heavens and mate with their hats! After the male falcon has left a deposit of sperm, the 'scientists' collect it for use in the artificial insemination of female falcons.

Don Williams is a corporate man at Frito-Lay, Inc in Dallas, Texas. His title? Vice-President in charge of Flavor Chemists. During the course of his average day, he is required to taste at least 1 lb of potato chips.

Michael Stechnicki has common, and sometimes un-common, scents. He extracts, refines, condenses and bottles the scent of bear, deer, squirrel and, of course, skunk in addition to the scent of other wild animals. His 'fragrances' are then bottled and sold, not on perfumery shelves in elegant department stores, but in his sportsman's store in Latrobe, Pennsylvania. Purchased by hunters, the scents are used to train dogs to follow a trail. Stechnicki has been in the scent business for nearly 50 years. He certainly must have a nose for business.

A job which doesn't seem to have much of a future is that of chicken shooter. That's the person who operates a cannon, firing dead chickens at aircraft to determine what kind of damage occurs when a bird collides with it.

## John Harrison has the kind of job most people dream about: he is an ice cream taster. His tongue is insured for $1,000.

Stephen May, of Los Angeles, is an animal chauffeur. His uniform comprises a natty bow tie and a shirt embroidered with the legend 'Pet Limo – we escort your pet to the vet'. The limousine is equipped for the most discerning animal: blanket-covered floor, 8 in color television, a spray of silk flowers and stereo speakers.

On one occasion, Stephen May was chauffeur to a most unusual wedding guest – a boxer (of the canine kind!) wearing a dress with pink flowers. The dog preceded the bride down the aisle. On another occasion the chauffeur had to babysit 2 Dobermans. Their owner asked him to entertain them – by taking them to the movies.

King Alfonso of Spain was so tone deaf that he employed someone known as the Anthem Man, whose task was to alert his Royal master whenever the Spanish national anthem was being played. Only then did the King know when to stand up and salute.

# Sports mad

*There's world-wide interest in the fascinating field of frog jumping.*

When the Calaveras County Frog Jumping Contest was first held on May 21 1928, 5,000 peopled attended.

It is still the most popular event of its kind, drawing huge crowds, and entries from as far afield as South America, England, Germany, Australia, Canada and Mexico. Preliminary contests are held throughout the world in the annual selection of an International Champion.

The distance of the jump is measured in a straight line from the starting point to the wet mark left by the frog's belly on its third jump. The world record is 19 ft 3⅛ in. From the thousands of frogs entered in the hundreds of qualifying trials, only the top 20 are allowed to compete in the International Finals.

Competitors can either bring their own frog or take advantage of the 'rent-a-frog' offer. This competition really is one jump ahead of the rest.

**For some people, eating is an art. For others, it is simply a necessity, to which they don't pay much attention. But to one guy, commonly referred to as 'the Exterminator' eating means disgusting all those who watch you in action. The Exterminator once ate 28 cockroaches in 4 minutes.**

The Neusiedlersee is the third largest lake in Europe, covering an area of nearly 150 square miles, in the southeastern corner of Austria. Every August it is the venue for one of the most bizarre events in Europe. Hundreds of people from several countries arrive at Moorbisch, a tiny village on the Austrian shore. They come to race on the lake, not by boat or ski, but on foot. This event requires its contestants to walk across the lake from Moorbisch to Illmitz, 2 miles away on the opposite shore.

How do they do it? The Neusiedlersee is not only one of the largest lakes in Europe but, with an average depth of under 6 ft, it's also one of the shallowest (on very windy days the lake is blown one side to the other and every century or so it completely disappears!). The contestants slog, trudge, tread and flounder across the narrow strait. The current record is 49 minutes and 35 seconds. Those who take part in the race say it may not be walking on water, but it's the next best thing.

The fishermen's tale about 'The one that got away' is never told in Cottonwood, Minnesota. In the Annual Fishless Derby ice-fishing competition held there everyone wins – except the angler who is unlucky enough actually to catch a fish.

Tom Shufflebottom, an English pig farmer, holds an annual Worm Charming Championship. His own world-famous charming technique involves wiggling a pitchfork back and forth in the ground to create a 'local earthquake' which, he believes, drives worms to the surface. He once raised over 500 worms in this way. Other techniques include playing the clarinet, having a horse stomp its hooves on the ground and using liquid detergent to make the worms itch and scratch their way to the surface. The latter method, however, is illegal and those found using it are banned for life.

*These sporting types could charm the worms right out of the ground - and frequently do.*

# Sports mad

Surfing in the desert, 500 miles from the ocean, is the latest craze at Big Surf, Tempe, in Arizona. The surf is produced by wave-making machines installed in a huge lake-like pool.

**Newton Smith, of Cuero, Texas, once shot 3 deer with one bullet. His single shot passed through the first deer and struck the second, which was standing behind the first. The bullet then passed through the second deer and struck the third, which was unfortunate enough to be standing 15 ft behind the first 2.**

MUDWALKING, or *wadlopen*, is a popular sport in Holland. It is held at low tide from May through September. The walkers have to move fast through the mud towards islands as far as 10 miles offshore, and it sometimes involves walking waist-deep in water. One participant described it as 'something like snowshoeing on balloons made of yogurt, only messier'.

Dawson City, Yukon, Canada, is the home of the annual Klondike Outhouse Race. Contestants push, pull, drag or carry their outhouses through the streets of the town. Prizes are awarded for the fastest, most humorous, best dressed and worst outhouses. One year the award for the Most Humorous went to the 'Shorts Snitchers', who decorated their outhouse with underwear that they had stolen from local officials.

Alice Springs is in the middle of the driest area of Australia. Yet local boating enthusiasts can still enjoy the thrill of the race – at nearby Henley-on-Todd, the world's only waterless regatta. 'Rowers' can compete in 'eights', during which the crew members run in line inside a bottomless racing shell. Alternatively they can join in the 'Oxford Tubs', in which team members sit in half a 44-gallon drum and propel it along rails by rowing with small shovels. There is even a surf ski rescue, where a lifesaver rescues a 'drowning' damsel, and a sea battle, the outcome of which is usually controversial because, so far, neither boat has ever sunk.

In some races the boats are perhaps a little suspect – they must be made of old beer cans. This idea originated in Darwin in 1974, when the first Beer Can Regatta attracted 60 entrants and thousands of cheering spectators, who sportingly did their best to ensure that there were enough beer cans for the next year's competition. The floats can be of any design but must be built of beer cans which have been opened and emptied by the contestants themselves. While the can used must be in more or less its original state, most of the entrants usually find themselves in an inebriated condition when the races come to an end.

## IT'S A FACT

The tallest man to have played basketball was Sulieman Ali Nashnush (born 1943), who in 1962 played for the Libyan national team. He stood 2.45m (8 ft).

**A Rotten Sneaker Contest is held annually in Montpelier, Vermont. In order to qualify, each entrant must have two particularly smelly sneakers – and a nose for the repulsive.**

At the wildlife park in Eatonville, Washington, enthusiasts can enjoy the Slug Derby. Fortunately, this is nowhere near Harrisville in New Hampshire, where the Annual Zucchini (courgette) Festival is held. The judges here not only have to be knowledgeable enough to determine the winner of the best peaceful use of a zucchini and the best zucchini look-alike, but also to award the somewhat dubious title of Ms Zucchini.

In Deming, New Mexico, the Great American Duck Race is held every August. The festival features a Duck Queen and Darling Duckling contest. Ducks have a special day in Nehalem, Oregon, too. An Annual Duck Day is staged in February, featuring Duck Bingo, a waddle contest and a duck-calling contest. Competitors do not have to be quackers, but it helps. The competitions take place in any weather – fair or fowl.

Wynard, Saskatchewan, hosts the World Championship Chicken Chariot Races. Chariots weighing 1 lb are attached to the tails of the birds, who race down a 15-meter enclosed track.

**Snail racing fanatics must be quick off the mark to stay ahead of the game. Gallic gastropod breeder and trainer Antoine Vallarejo puts his tiny charges through a rigorous training program that involves obstacle walks, tender words of encouragement and bribes of lettuce.**

The World's Shortest Saint Patrick's Day Parade is held on March 17 in Maryville, Missouri. The parade gets shorter every year so that it can break its own record. One day, presumably, it will disappear altogether.

For insomniacs there are the World Pillow Fighting Championships in Kenwood, California – a much more energetic way to get tired than counting sheep!

In Manchester, New Hampshire, secretaries have a Typewriter Tossing Contest.

# Food for thought

One of the most popular eggplant (aubergine) dishes of the Middle East is named Iman Bayaldi, 'The Priest has fainted'. According to legend, a holy man was visiting the home of a renowned beauty. As she was about to serve him a delectable meal of eggplants, her veil slipped, revealing her face. To this day no one knows whether it was her face or the eggplant which was responsible for the priest's collapse.

A worm's dried weight is 72 per cent protein. According to Worm Concern, in Southern California, this makes worms the perfect ingredient for such tasty morsels as Worm Surprise Cake and Worm omelets. Worm Concern sells a cookery book in which a typical recipe begins: 'Just mix 1½ lb ground earthworms ...'. The book has yet to reach the best-seller list.

Anton Fitz, a star musician at the brilliant court of Mannheim in Germany, died at the age of 27. The cause? He ate too many spiders, which he claimed tasted just like strawberries. Perhaps he would have enjoyed dining with Hal Irby, of Austin, Texas, who is the ultimate omnivore. He eats virtually anything – black widow spiders, mice, live fish, scorpions, lizards, brown ground snakes. He started his dubious 'gourmet' adventures as a child and claims that nothing he has eaten has made him sick.

**The most expensive food in the world is not caviare but First Choice Black Périgord truffle, which can be found at Harrods in London, England, and currently costs £25 per 12.5g jar.**

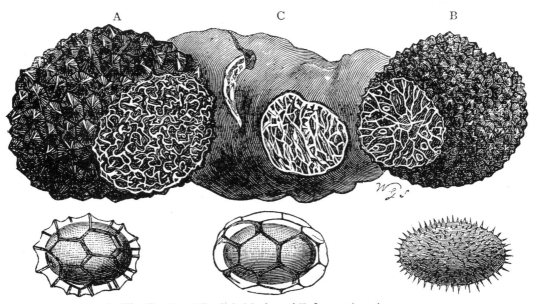

A, The Truffle of English Markets (*Tuber æstivum*).
B, ,, ,, French ,, ( ,, *melanosporum*).
C, ,, ,, Italian ,, ( ,, *magnatum*).

Thomas Jefferson wrote America's Declaration of Independence and is credited as the father of American democracy. It should also be noted that he is credited with introducing spaghetti, French fries, and other foods to America. He also invented an automatic pen that made copies of documents in his handwriting as he wrote them.

## Eli's Chicago's Finest Cheesecake provided a 2,000 lb cheesecake for Bill Clinton's presidential inauguration. The cheesecake's 10 layers were assembled by forklifts.

In the Museum of Ham in Spain, hundreds of hams hang above other pork products displayed in glass cases. The Spaniards take their pork so seriously that apart from going to the museum, they have also been flocking to see a film called *'Jamon Jamon' (Ham Ham)*. At its violent climax, two rivals in a love triangle club each other with legs of ham until one falls dead in the sand. The victor would probably be found guilty of hamicide!

El Vez, the Mexican self-proclaimed Elvis, was not to be outdone when the United States issued Elvis stamps. He offered his own line of stamps depicting his well known Elvis pose. But El Vez decided to go one better than the US Post Office. His stamps have chili sauce-flavored backings in three flavors, mild, medium and extra hot.

The first hot dogs, called 'Dachshund Sausages', were sold on Coney Island, New York, in 1871 – without the buns. The vendor would simply plop a 'dog' into the customer's hands. Some vendors even gave their customers white gloves with which to hold the 'Dachshund'!

Large ears and radiators are both names of pasta! Cappelletti are little hats, fettuccine are small ribbons, gemelli are twins, radiatori are little radiators, orecchioni are large ears, linguini are small tongues, occhi di trota are trout's eyes, and occhi di lupo are wolf's eyes.

The largest item on any menu in the world is probably roast camel, sometimes served at Bedouin wedding feasts. The camel is stuffed with a sheep's carcass, which is stuffed with chickens, which are stuffed with fish, which are stuffed with eggs. The groom probably spends the evening hoping his new mother-in-law doesn't get the hump!

> **IT'S A FACT**
>
> **The record for oyster eating was set in 1975, when a 48-year-old Florida man devoured 588 in a mere 17.5 minutes. The same year a Washington man poured 424 clams down his throat in only 8 minutes.**
>
> **The prune-sitting record set at the annual Prairie Dog Chili Cook-off in Grand Prairie, Texas, is 30 ft 8 in.**

In Jerusalem famous foods and cooks are immortalized in street names. Suq El Lahhamin, for example, means Butcher Market. The street names, and the products sold in them, have remained unchanged for centuries. Suq Khan ez-Zeit means the Olive Oil Market and there is a Street of Herbs. All of the streets in this section of Jerusalem are worth a visit, except perhaps Malquisinat: 'The Street of Bad Cooking'.

# Remarkable buildings

Deep in the heart of the Alps is a mountain called La Mer de Glace, or Sea of Ice. George Cloret dug a tunnel into its heart and cut out an apartment, complete with kitchen, bathroom and bedroom. The apartment is fully furnished, with a stove, refrigerator, bed and dresser, a living-room suite and an upright piano – all carved out of ice.

One of the largest tombs in the world was that built for King Mausolus of Halicarnassus by his wife Artemisia. One of the Seven Ancient Wonders, it was built to be seen at a distance by passing ships. When finished the tomb was 140 ft high and 440 ft across. It was topped by a pyramid and the statues of Artemisia and Mausolus in a chariot. Unfortunately Mausolus never made it to his tomb.

*Have you ever wondered how mausoleums came to be so named?*

Artemisia, overwrought with grief at his death, poured Mausolus' ashes into a cup of wine and drank him. Perhaps the word mausoleum, which comes from the King's name, should have been applied to a kind of cocktail rather than a tomb.

The Great Pyramid of Cheops in Egypt covers 13 acres and contains 2.3 million limestone blocks, each weighing 2½ tons. If all the blocks were cut into 1 ft square segments and laid end to end, they would form a line nearly 17,000 miles long.

In winter, there's a cool little bed and breakfast to be had in Jukkasjarvi in the north of Sweden, at the Arctic Hotel, though the managers foresee a bit of a meltdown come spring because the place is made entirely of ice. The furniture in the 6,000 sq ft, one-room lodge is made of snow. Each snowy bed is covered with reindeer pelts.

While it has no showers or hot tubs, the lodge does come equipped with its own toilet, bar and chapel, in which, presumably, guests pray for heat. Although temperatures outside average 10-15° Fahrenheit below zero, the hotel, when occupied, heats up to a cozy 30° Fahrenheit. Unfortunately, the one thing you can't do during those arctic nights is cuddle up in front of the fireplace.

An environmentally conscious builder in Rockport, Massachusetts, constructed a home entirely of recycled newspaper. Should you suspect this architectural wonder of being a bit flimsy, you'd be wrong. Each of its walls is plied with 215 reinforced layers of newsprint. Naturally all the furniture is also made of paper – there's even a desk made of newspapers reporting Lindbergh's historic flight. So come on into the Paper House, a place that can really rub off on you (if you scrape against the ink on the walls). But remember to leave your matches and cigarette lighters on the porch – it's part of the owner's fire insurance policy!

**The largest hotel in the world is the Excaliber Hotel and Casino in Las Vegas, Nevada (above). It stands on a 117-acre plot, houses 4,032 suites and employs a staff of over 4,500. The hotel includes 11 restaurants and some 15 pools.**

The most expensive hotel is the Hotel Bel-Air in Los Angeles, California. In 1989 it was sold for $1.2 million per room to the Sekitei Kaihatsu Company of Tokyo, Japan.

# Remarkable buildings

*If you want to get a head - go to the Paris Catacombs, home to the remains of 6 million people.*

Beneath the streets of Paris there are 300 km of passageways: the Paris Catacombs. When the city was being built, the stone needed to construct houses, pave roads and bridge the river all came from limestone quarries beneath the site. Eventually the buildings began to collapse so the digging had to stop.

But Paris continued to expand and by 1786 the space problem had become so acute that the city's leaders decided to empty the ancient cemeteries and build on them. The bones were dug up, moved in the dead of night in funeral carts accompanied by priests and relocated in the vast unused quarries beneath the streets of the Latin Quarter.

The value of the cemetery land offset any qualms the enterprising Parisians might have had about disturbing the dead. Over a period of several decades the occupants of most of Paris' principal cemeteries were unceremoniously dumped in huge piles 150 ft below the city's teeming streets. It wasn't until the reign of Louis Napoleon that some thought was given to the desecration. Workmen and artisans were sent below to straighten things out. They decorated miles and miles of walls with bones and skulls.

Today Paris has a population of 9 million people above ground. Beneath its streets the skeletons of another 6 million make the most bizarre mosaic tourist attraction in the world.

The most impressive structure in the town of Hall, in Austria, is the Church of St Niklaus. Its foundations were laid in 1281 but its spectacular Waldauf Chapel was not decorated until some time later.

Waldauf was a knight of the Emperor Maximilian I. He traveled quite extensively and during one voyage there was a terrible storm. Fearing for his life, Waldauf vowed that, should he be spared, he would build a chapel and fill it with precious relics.

The storm died down, Waldauf was spared and the bones of saints became fair game. Over the years he managed to bag himself quite a collection. Skeletons from Austria, Germany and France can be found in the Waldauf Chapel. But he didn't want the place to look like a house of bones so he had each of the relics wrapped in silk. He even placed some skeletons, robed and crowned, on a throne. The Waldauf Chapel is one of the most bizarre sights in Christendom.

The Winchester Mystery House is a 160-room mansion which was never intended to be completed. With its 10,000 windows, 47 fire places, 3 elevators and spectacular Victorian garden, it was the home of Mrs Sarah L. Winchester, heiress to the rifle fortune, from 1884 until her death in 1922.

Upon the death of her husband and young daughter, Mrs Winchester had been convinced by a spiritualist medium that their lives had been taken by spirits – the spirits of those killed by the 'Gun that Won the West'. She was convinced that she would share their fate unless she began building a mansion for the spirits – a mansion on which work must never be completed.

With an income of $1,000 per day from her fortune, Sarah began building in 1884. The sounds of carpenters' tools could be heard 24 hours a day for almost 38 years. The resultant $5,000,000 architectural curiosity has modern heating, sewer systems and gas lights that operate at the touch of a button.

It has exquisite hand-painted inlaid parquet floors throughout, gold and silver chandeliers and Tiffany art glass windows. Sarah even built a spooky staircase leading nowhere, demented doors that open into walls, windows in the floors for watching the weirdness, escape hatches, secret passageways and blind cupboards.

As if the building wasn't peculiar enough, Sarah was obsessed with the number 13. In the sewing room she insisted on 13 windows and 13 doors. There are 13 bathrooms, 13 hooks in every cupboard and 13 candles in every chandelier. There were even 13 parts to her will, which she signed 13 times.

**The Central soccer stadium in Rio de Janeiro has a 10 ft wide and 8 ft deep moat surrounding the field. It was built to keep back riotous fans – it's thought that the Professional Referees' Association financed its construction. Why don't fans simply swim the moat to reach their favorite player? It's rumored to be stocked with piranhas. So far, no one's tested the water.**

# Remarkable buildings

In Ebbw Vale, deep in the heartland of Wales, pride of place goes to the ominous triumphal arch standing above all who enter the Welsh Garden Festival. It is 30 ft high and cost close to a quarter of a million dollars. The Arc de Triomphe in Paris and London's Admiralty Arch may be bigger and better – but unlike Ebbw Vale's arch they can't give you the time of day.

Two hundred years ago, the Mayor of Amberg, in Germany, decided that marriage should be restricted to the landed gentry, which naturally included him and his friends but excluded practically everyone else in town. To qualify for a marriage license young lovers had to prove that they owned property.

The owner of number 8 Seminargasse, decided to take pity on the town's landless lovebirds and agreed to sell them his house for a low price, thus making them landowners and enabling them to marry. Less the romantic than the opportunist, the owner always bought the house back the next day for less than he had sold it.

Since that time, number 8 Seminargasse has been sold and repurchased thousands of times more than any other house in the world. Although the law has been repealed the tradition continues, and the house, with its single bedroom, now qualifies as the smallest honeymoon hotel on the planet.

In 1618, not far from Salzburg, in Austria, Archbishop Marcus Sitticus built Schloss Hellbrunn, where he entertained unsuspecting guests to sumptuous banquets.

The Archbishop was intrigued by water. The grounds of Schloss Hellbrunn feature

exquisite grottos populated by sculptures of moving mythical creatures which spit water; there was an organ, powered by water, whose music accompanied the movements of the wooden inhabitants, and an entire miniature village, also powered by water. But that wasn't all. While watching this amazing display, bemused guests would suddenly be drenched by sprays hidden in the trees: the entire palace had been designed so that the Archbishop could douse his guests! His *pièce de resistance* was an outside dining-table where each of the chairs (except for the Archbishop's) was fitted with a barely perceptible nozzle in the seat. Etiquette dictated that until the Archbishop got to his feet, guests had to stay seated, so his friends would squirm and wriggle through each course, while their seemingly oblivious host slowly ate his venison, drank his wine and chatted with whoever could still carry on a conversation.

For many people a weekend at Schloss Hellbrunn was the highlight of the social calendar: apparently the only thing not dampened by the Archbishop's antics was their spirit. Almost 400 years later this water playground still entertains, amazes and drenches its steady stream of visitors.

**In Sacramento, California, the architects of the Best Catalog Store have found a way to beat earthquakes: they produced a building that comes apart at the seams – every day. Each morning at 9 o'clock a huge section of the store's front cracks open as if it has been hit by the 'Big One'. The owners of Best hope customers will slip through the cracks in record numbers.**

# Remarkable buildings

Publisher, art collector and movie producer William Randolph Hearst envisioned his weekend ranch retreat as an estate unlike any other – an architectural masterpiece displaying his vast and varied art collections. He called his San Simeon residence La Cuesta Encantada – The Enchanted Hill – and opened its art-filled halls and guest houses to many of the most famous, influential and creative figures of the early 20th century.

To design and build his hilltop castle, Hearst chose San Francisco architect Julia Morgan, and planning began in 1919. San Simeon grew to be a twin-towered 115-room castle with 3 guest houses, indoor and outdoor swimming pools, gardens, tennis courts, and even a zoo with 120 varieties of wildlife.

Hearst indulged his enthusiasm for art and art collecting, and Morgan frequently designed rooms around a particular piece of furniture or art. Changes were made so frequently that no complete set of drawings exist. He bought a 10th-century Spanish cloister, had it dismantled stone by stone, transported in 10,700 wooden crates and reassembled at San Simeon. The outdoor mosaic-lined Neptune swimming pool, more than 100 ft long, was rebuilt 3 times before Hearst was satisfied.

Hearst's guest list included journalists, European royalty, Hollywood celebrities and athletes. Charles Chaplin, Winston Churchill, Greta Garbo, W.C. Fields, Charles Lindbergh and Clark Gable were just a few of those who received invitations to San Simeon.

But, no matter who they were, once they arrived at San Simeon, they were all treated the same. When the big brass cowbell announced dinner, guests had to be seated – latecomers would be sent away. Ketchup and mustard bottles stood on the 40 ft table side by side with Georgian silver. There was no privacy – if Hearst overheard a conversation he considered newsworthy, it would appear in the following day's paper.

**Despite great wealth, and a reputation as a marvelous host, Hearst expected his guests to pay for their own phone calls and presented everyone with a bill at the end of their stay.**

*Rumor has it that there's a horse at the palatial Chantilly stables who looks as if he owns the place...*

Louis Henri, Duke of Bourbon, was fascinated with reincarnation – and horses. Somewhere along the way his two interests converged and he became convinced that he was going to be reincarnated as a horse. So, when he came to design a palace he built stables and riding arenas which were more spacious and luxurious than the palace itself. No expense was spared because the Duke hoped to live many lifetimes in these stables and he felt he would more than get his money's worth. Today Chantilly Castle is one of the world's leading equestrian centers. There is no proof that the Duke is a resident, though they do say there is one horse that walks around the place as if he owns it.

The *Mayflower*, which took the pilgrims to America, was owned by the Dutch company, Amstel, and was a wine-merchant's ship leased to the highest bidder. Eventually she outlived her usefulness and was put up for auction. She was purchased by a man named Russell, who took her up the Thames in 1642 on what would be her last voyage. She was dismantled near Marlow and her timbers were taken to Russell's farm in Old Jordan's Village, where she was reconstructed as a barn.

Nearly 100 years later William Penn, former landlord of Delaware, New Jersey and Pennsylvania, nearly blind, destitute and living in England, requested to be buried near the old barn on the hill, unconscious of the fact that it, too, had played a part in the future of the Colonies. He now rests in the shadow of the old barn, formerly known as *The Mayflower*.

# Crazy collections

**M**unich has a collection of over 2,000 chamber pots of all shapes, sizes and ages. There is a clay pot manufactured in Holland in 1500; exquisite porcelain pots made in China and Japan; a pure silver pot made in 1840; a pot belonging to King Ludwig II; art deco pots, musical pots – and one made in Britain during World War II with Hitler's face painted on the bottom and the words 'Have this on Old Nasty' printed round the rim!

**I**n the popular seaside resort of Yarmouth in England the Howkins Museum houses what may be the world's only stamp room. Its creator, Albert Schaeffer, began his career as a circus clown. From time to time he also stood in for the acrobats. One day he took a nasty fall and broke a couple of bones. To occupy the time in hospital he started to collect, lick and plaster stamps on the objects around him. Later, in his London apartment, he began making

designs out of stamps. He took all the Vs from a stamp featuring King George V, and made scales out of them, which he used to cover a model fish. During World War II, when the city was being bombed nightly, he refused to leave, passing the dark, dangerous nights licking stamps under his dining-room table and sticking them on anything which didn't move. Over the years every object in his apartment, from the piano to a portrait of George Washington, was covered with stamps.

After his death his collection of stamp-covered ornaments, pictures, windows, tables, chairs, desks and carpets was sold and taken to Yarmouth. Unfortunately the move was ill-conceived. During the 100-mile trip from London tens of thousands of stamps were shaken loose, covering the floor of the truck. When the doors were opened, many of the stamps blew away in the wind.

Coincidentally, another circus clown read about the tragedy and volunteered to restore the collection. At the age of 81 Arthur Van Norman decided to spend the rest of his life re-pasting the stamps that had fallen off Albert Schaeffer's collection, ultimately re-covering every square inch of the room. His efforts would undoubtedly have earned Schaeffer's stamp of approval.

**The Museum of Modern Art in New York City hung Matisse's 'Le Bateau' upside-down for 47 days before an art student noticed the error.**

Berlin's Escape Museum contains some of the extraordinary cont-raptions of the lucky few who succeeded in crossing the Berlin Wall from East to West Germany.

Among the more amazing construc-tions is a home-made airplane built by a Czech student, who escaped by flying over the Wall. The propeller had been laboriously carved from wood and everything but the engine, gas tank and wheels were hand made or constructed from recycled materials. On a wing and a prayer, he flew at a height of 400 meters to avoid both radar and the ground troops' gunfire.

Another exhibit features a home-made submarine, which was successfully navigated from East to West. One of the most extraordinary displays is Johan Gerich's mini-car in which he success-fully smuggled out his fiancée in a hollowed-out passenger seat.

Berlin is the only city in the world with a museum dedicated to man's will to escape tyranny.

The German Tobacco and Cigar Museum in Bunde is a smoker's paradise. It comprises 7 rooms containing hundreds of pipes from all over the world, many dating back several centuries. There are pipes belonging to the famous, such as Johann Sebastian Bach, as well as tobacco tins, boxes, cigarette-making machines and, in pride of place, the world's largest cigar – almost 6 ft long, and containing enough tobacco to provide 600 hours of smoking delight.

Amsterdam's Piggy Bank Museum contains 12,000 piggy banks from every period of history. There are gold and silver ones and some with most delicate engravings. As well as traditional pig-shaped banks, there are primitive earthenware turtles, Taj Mahals and Winston Churchill look-alikes. There are also a number of mechanical pieces, including a magician, who makes the money disappear under his hat.

The Smithsonian Museum in Washington has a fascinating collection which includes: an original Edison light bulb – which still works; Teddy Roosevelt's teddy bear; a full-grown male gorilla, preserved in formaldehyde; 10 specimens of dinosaur excrement; air sickness bags; trimmings from Abraham Lincoln's hearse; Tom Thumb's miniature piano; an aluminum violin; the Luckenheimer Peggy – a round pill box-like container that opens to reveal a single small spike, where one could store a half-chewed wad of gum for a future chew; and a texture meter – an early 20th-century device for testing the tenderness of shelled peas by recording their rate of squash.

**For the jaded tourist who has been everywhere and done everything, perhaps the last word in excitement can be found in Kissimmee, Florida. There, enthusiasts can visit the Tupperware Museum, where they can enjoy the intriguing history of food containers.**

The Nut Museum in Old Lyme, Connecticut, holds a huge collection of nutcrackers – including one 10 ft long. There is also a 35 lb coconut (perhaps that is why the 10 ft long nutcracker was made!). The price of admission includes one of any type of nut.

# Ancient worlds

In 1748 Alcubierre, engineer to the King of Naples, was inspecting an ancient tunnel used for carrying water from the Sarno River to Pompeii. He sank a pole into the ground and discovered a hole. Lowering himself into it, he discovered a city: the ancient city of Pompeii.

Then he found the body of a Pompeian, still clutching a handful of gold. The body was nearly 2,000 years old. It was the first of hundreds of bodies to be discovered, for in this city, preserved by the ash and stone which engulfed it when the volcano Vesuvius erupted on August 24 79AD, the remains of the inhabitants were also preserved, hermetically sealed so that every detail could be observed nearly two millenia later.

The ash and stone from the volcano had acted as a mold. As the victims' skin decayed, their bones remained in a tomb which formed a cast of their features in the minutest detail.

By pouring plaster in the 'tombs' the bones were encased and the exact form and position of each person who had succumbed to Vesuvius' might could once again be seen: people huddled against walls, a man chained in a dungeon, a dog writhing in agony, a father reaching in vain for his young son. A society frozen in time by the heat of a mighty volcano.

In Memphis, the ancient capital of Egypt, there was a cemetery specifically for bulls. It was known as the Serapeum and was the burial place of the sacred Apis bulls, which were deified and honored above all other animals by the Egyptians. The Serapeum was discovered and then excavated by the French archaeologist, Auguste-Edouard Mariette, in 1851. More than 60 tombs were found, containing the carefully mummified bodies of the bulls, enclosed in enormous stone sarcophagi.

**Eratosthenes lived from 276-194 BC. In measuring the radius of the earth – without precise instruments – he came within 1 per cent of the correct value. He found the answer to be 6,350 km, compared with today's average space craft-determined value of 6,371 km.**

The Mayan Indians rose to artistic and intellectual heights unmatched in the ancient world. Their knowledge of astronomy was particularly profound. Not until the 20th century could Western scientists predict eclipses with the accuracy with which the Mayans could a millenium before.

The Mayans kept a very accurate track of time. Their history began in 3,113 BC and they counted the number of days that passed since. This was done on a calendar consisting of kins (days), uinals (20 days), tuns (360 days), the katun (7,200 days) and the baktun (144,000 days). They were able to keep track of the days with a mathematical system that was as simple as it was efficient. Using only 3 symbols: a dot for 1, a bar for 5, and a shell shape for 0, the Mayans could calculate in hundreds of millions. In fact, they are known to have been the first civilization to use the concept of zero, 1,000 years before the rest of the world.

But although they constructed cities for up to 40,000 people and pyramids larger than those of Egypt, the Mayans could never build a simple arch, never developed the wheel and never invented weaponry more sophisticated than the spear. In fact, this single failure to innovate led to their demise. When the Europeans reached South America with their weaponry, neither the Mayans' ability to predict eclipses nor to count to a million beginning with 0 could save them!

Tutankhamun was 9 years old when he became King of Egypt. He died only 9 years later – some say he was murdered. The whereabouts of his tomb remained a secret for over 3,000 years until Howard Carter discovered it in 1922. Ever since it was opened the Curse of King Tutankhamun is said to have visited those who desecrated it.

The day Carter broke the tomb's seal a violent sand storm blew and a hawk was seen flying westward. The Egyptian workers present at the time said that this was the spirit of the King.

The first victim of the 'curse' was Lord Carnarvon, the man responsible for financing the operation. During a visit to the tomb he was bitten by a mosquito. The resulting infection killed him. At the moment of his death all the lights of Cairo went out. Later, doctors examining the mummy found a fresh scab mark on the cheek corresponding exactly to Carnarvon's mosquito bite. The following year his brother died of peritonitis.

Soon afterwards the American railroad tycoon J.G. Gould, who visited the tomb, caught pneumonia and died. The next year the Egyptian Prince Ali Farmi Bey, whose family claims to be Tutankhamun's descendants and who participated in the excavation of the jewels, was found murdered in his London hotel room. His brother later committed suicide, as did Richard Bethel, who helped catalog the contents of the tomb. Altogether, more than a dozen people fell victim to the Pharaoh's alleged curse. Then, suddenly, it stopped: no more sudden deaths, no more nasty accidents for 40 years.

But in 1966, when the Tutankhamun relics were to be shipped from Cairo to Paris, the curator in charge of shipping the exhibits started having recurring dreams that if he allowed the jewels to leave the country, he would die. On the day of the shipment he was hit by a car and killed; the plane nearly crashed on its way to France; 3 of the 12 crew members died violent deaths within 12 months of the shipment. Curse or coincidence?

*Howard Carter and Lord Carnarvon at the entrance to Tutankhamun's tomb. Were they the victims of a 'curse'?*

# Spooky tales

When Charles VI premiered an opera in Paris in 1852, some said it was a 'smashing success', others said it was cursed. On the first night Mafiani, the leading tenor, was just singing the words 'Oh God, smash him', referring to the play's villain, when he caught a glimpse of a stage hand watching from the catwalk high above. The stage hand instantly fell to his death.

The next night the terrified tenor fixed his eyes on an empty box seat throughout the show. But, just as he sang, 'Oh, God smash him' a late arrival entered the box. As his eyes met the tenor's, he suddenly grabbed his chest and collapsed from a heart attack, The late arrival had made an early departure.

The producers panicked, perhaps believing that death 'comes in threes'. But Mafiani assured them that he had a solution to the problem. He would simply stare at the floor during the fateful aria. Just as he came to the lethal line for a third time, a musician in the orchestra happened to play off-key. By reflex, Mafiani glared at him as the words left his mouth. The unlucky violinist died instantly. The opera has never been performed since.

*The Paris Opera House, where Mafiani, the tenor, had a devastating effect.*

University Professor Dr Steven Kaplan has set up a Research Centre in Elmhurt, Queens, New York, to give help with emotional problems to – vampires! The professor, who has himself drunk blood, says that vampires call in regularly on his telephone hot line 'Nightline'. He insists that he has seen aspiring vampires have dentists sharpen their front teeth, that he has interviewed at least 50 real vampires and guesses that there are hundreds more throughout the world. He feels that vampires are an endangered species, much in need of a support group. Perhaps instead of 'Nightline' his service should be called 'Bloodline'.

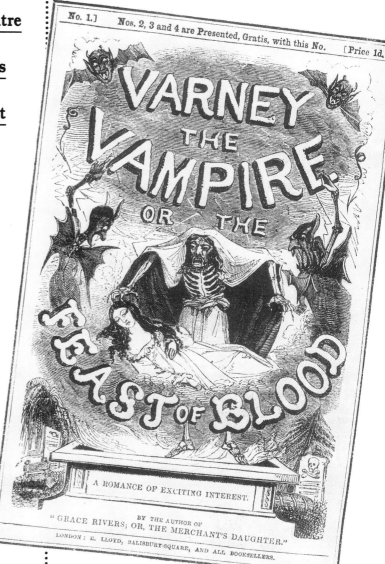

Pluckley is the most haunted village in England, with over a dozen ghosts roaming the streets. On a dark night, visitors to the picture-postcard village could meet the red lady, who searches the local graveyard for her lost child; the screaming man, who yells for help from the clay pit into which he fell to his death; a highwayman, who has been seen with a sword thrust into his stomach; the schoolmaster, who hanged himself; the monk, who likes to talk to passers-by; the mistress of Rose Court, who can sometimes be seen chatting to the monk; and a gypsy, who died when her pipe set her aflame. There's also a mysterious coach, which charges through the town and disappears as fast as it comes.

# Spooky tales

The body of the 17th-century devout religious emancipator Roger Williams was eaten by a tree. Williams died in 1683 and was buried in a poorly marked grave at his home; 56 years later, while excavating another grave, grave-diggers accidentally broke

*Roger Williams*

[*Supposed Portrait.*]

into his coffin, exposing the bones. Then in 1860 Stephen Randall, a descendant of Williams, ordered a workman to exhume the remains from the Providence, Rhode Island, plot and transfer them to a more suitable tomb. But the excavation yielded only a few badly rusted coffin nails and scraps of rotten wood.

The workmen, however, did find something extraordinary. The root of a nearby apple tree lay exactly where the remains should have been, and it had taken the shape of Williams' body. As it grew, the root had apparently encountered Williams' skull and followed the path of least resistance, inching down the side of his head, backbone, hip and legs, molding itself closely to the contours of his body. The corpse itself was gone: absorbed into the tree.

The human-shaped root was removed for safekeeping and today is on display at the Rhode Island Historical Society in Providence.

Some people believe in ghosts, others do not. The American Government, however, is in no doubt as to their existence. The US department of Commerce in Washington DC has issued a list of haunted houses and legendary ghosts, including Haw Branch Plantation, Virginia, 'a happy haunting ground for a myriad of ghosts'; Musical Wonder House, Maine, where 'spirits chatter'; the Myrtles Plantation, Louisiana, which is 'haunted by a French governess, who appears to peer into sleeping faces in the bedroom'; St Maurice Plantation where 'spirits noisily turn calendar pages'; Westover Plantation, Virginia, 'home to the ghost of Evelyn Byrd, who died of a broken heart'; and Woodburn, Delaware, where they say 'a wine-sipping ghost empties decanters in the dining-room'.

During the reign of Henry VIII in 16th-century England John Styles was the Catholic priest of St Mary's Church, Woodford. At that time people were losing their heads for professing a belief in Catholicism and, not wanting to push his luck, Styles fled to Belgium. He took with him the church's most sacred possession, a gold chalice. Not long after his escape, he died in the monastery where he had taken refuge.

A few years later Styles' friend Andrew Powlett, who had become Anglican pastor of St Mary's, traveled to Belgium to recover the holy chalice. According to custom, he also retrieved John Styles' heart. The chalice was returned to the altar and the heart was entombed in the church. Over the centuries the chalice disappeared. John Styles and his heart were forgotten.

Then, in 1862, the St Mary's pastor saw, on several occasions, a ghost in the hallway of the rectory. It seemed to be hovering near a certain panel in the wall. The curious pastor examined the panel and found a secret cavity. Inside was the missing chalice. With it was a faded letter, which directed the reader to a pillar in the church. It said that if the mortar was chipped away, the heart of John Styles would be revealed. Intrigued by the note, the pastor located the pillar and went to work with hammer and chisel. In the center of the pillar was an ancient metal chest containing John Styles' heart. It is suspected that Andrew Powlett's restless spirit had led the pastor to the chalice and the heart. Perhaps he had hidden the chalice from those who would have desecrated it. *His* heart was in the right place – even if John Styles' wasn't!

In 1889 an English-woman and her daughter, on a visit to the Great Paris Exhibition, checked into one of the most lavish hotels. Each had her own room. The daughter wanted to take in the sights and sounds of the city immediately but her mother, tired after the trip, wanted to sleep. The girl accordingly went out alone, strolled down the Champs Elysées and saw the Eiffel Tower.

Six hours later she returned to her mother's room, only to find it empty, and no sign of her mother ever having been there. When she checked with the front desk they insisted that they had never seen her or her mother check in. The mother had vanished.

The desperate girl searched for weeks before finally returning to England. She died several years later in a mental

*A visit to the Paris exhibition, with its newly-erected Eiffel Tower, was an unforgettable experience for a young Englishwoman and her mother who 'vanished'.*

institution, distraught over having 'lost' her mother.

The explanation? After the daughter had gone sight-seeing, her mother complained to the hotel doctor that she felt ill. She had contracted the plague. The hotel officials were instructed to quash any news of this, lest everyone fled the city and the Great Exhibition ended in disaster. The mother's room was swiftly redecorated and another couple moved in. No one knows what happened to the mother but it is assumed she remained in France until she died.

# Trivia

Little is known of the Monster Gardens in Bomarzo, Italy, which was created in the 16th century by a Renaissance prince named Pier Francesco Orsini. The garden was his dream. Built on a steep hill overlooking the Tiber valley, it is an assortment of brutal and grotesque statues, seemingly not of this planet. Carved from huge volcanic boulders, they appear to have been shaped by some force other than man. In one part is a monstrous Hercules, ripping a man from stem to stern; in another section, a chapel decorated with symbols of death.

Elsewhere are a huge elephant trampling a Roman soldier, a castle on its back, dragons, bears, lions, a whale, a house on a serious tilt and a mermaid with a pot of flowers precariously balanced on her head. Carved into the hillside, overlooking this half-acre of weirdness, is a mammoth head with empty eye sockets and a gaping hole for a mouth into which one can walk, possibly never to return.

Judges for the Loo of the Year Contest in the UK spend their time visiting 1,300 toilets and discussing their merits. The much-coveted prize is a brass toilet seat, to be hung on the wall of the triumphant toilet. Ray Williams, a toilet attendant in Bristol, displayed to the judges his spotless cubicles, adorned by photographs of his many grandchildren. When he heard that the area prize had been won by a nearby toilet, he ruefully reflected that hanging baskets or plants might have helped in his quest for fame. Perhaps he should not be too disappointed – success may only be a flash in the pan.

## The world's largest urinal is in Poconas, Pennsylvania.

*The mammoth head in the gardens at Bomarzo. Is it waiting for a tasty visitor?*

The world's largest encyclopedia was the Yung Lo Ta Tien, or Great Standard of Yung Lo, compiled in China by order of the Emperor during the 15th century. It consisted of 22,937 books. Not surprisingly, only 3 copies of this vast work were ever made.

For the timekeeper at London's Tower Clock (often mistakenly referred to as Big Ben) accuracy is the name of the game. If the clock runs fast, the timekeeper places one or more pennies on the weight of the pendulum, thereby slowing it down. If it runs slow, he removes the coins.

How does the world's timekeeper know if the clock is running fast or slow? He calls the telephone company's timekeeping service. Tower Clock, responsible for the accuracy of national clocks in 150 nations, is kept precise by a call to the phone company and a pocket full of pence.

**'Big Ben' is not the name of the clock in the Tower at Westminster. The clock is called, appropriately, Tower Clock. Big Ben is the name of the 13½-ton chime that accompanies the clock.**

*Marking time at Westminster with the help of the Great Bell and the Quarter Bells.*

# Trivia

On January 15 1919 a tank on top of the Purity Distillery Company building in Boston, Massachusetts, exploded, unleashing 2 million gallons of hot syrup into the town. A 15 ft wave of molasses swamped the bustling streets, engulfing people and wrecking buildings. Hundreds of people and animals were seen wandering around covered in syrup. Wagons, cars and bicycles were scooped up and smashed and entire buildings collapsed under the weight. 21 people were killed and 150 injured by the time the sticky goo stopped oozing through Boston's boulevards.

Venice, the city beloved of honeymoon couples, was herself once married – to the sea. In 1,000 AD it was decided that Venice should marry the Adriatic. Thereafter, every Ascension Day, the Doge was rowed into the lagoon in his gondola and would drop a golden ring into the waves as a symbol of the marriage. The ceremony was abandoned in 1789.

The diamond is considered by many people to be the perfect mineral. Approximately 46,000 lb of earth must be excavated, mined and sifted to produce a single half-carat diamond of approximately 100 milligrams.

While the diamond is among the most durable of all known substances, it is composed of pure carbon and will burn if sufficiently heated with oxygen present. Under a blowtorch diamonds will be converted into graphite. In the San Francisco fire of 1906 temperatures reached as high as 2,200°F. Many San Franciscans returned to their burned-out homes expecting to find, if nothing else, their diamonds. But they, too, were burned.

## IT'S A FACT

From July 30 to August 1 1971, Command Service Module pilot Alfred M. Worden, (center below) on the US Apollo lunar mission, was 2,233.2 miles from the next nearest human being. That's the farthest any human has ever been from humanity.

John and Peter Collister are identical twins. Their wives, Pauline and Patricia, are also identical twins. They had a double wedding, complete with identical page-boys and bridesmaids. Their children are not only cousins but, genetically speaking, brother and sister.

The smelliest substance known to man is seleno-mercaptan ($C_4H_9SeH$). Of the 17,000 known substances scientists have been able to classify, this is reported to be the most foul smelling. Some say it conjures up images of rotting garbage, sewer gas and garlic rolled into one putrid package.

Most people have a skeleton in their closet. Henry Galiano, of New York, has a shop full. At his Manhatten store 'Maxilla and Mandible' he sells upper and lower jawbones – in sizes ranging from a mouse to a dinosaur – human kneecaps, assorted ribs, African giraffe skulls and skeletons of dogs, cats and snakes. The store is situated above the cellars where the bones are cleaned in huge cauldrons. Workers can be seen scraping off bits of gristle and there are aquariums filled with the carcasses of small animals such as bats and snakes covered with swarms of beetles who clean the bones. When the workers, both human and insect, have finished, the bones are bleached white, sealed with wax and are ready for assembly.

There are only 12 letters in the Hawaiian alphabet.

Did pirates have piercing good eyesight? Tradition has it that the old one-eyed bandits used to wear that one gold earring to improve their remaining eyesight. For centuries people laughed, but it turns out the pirates may have been right. Acupuncturists tell us that the pierced part of the earlobe is the spot which corresponds to human eyesight.

*Pirates might have known a thing or two when they pierced their ears.*

# Trivia

What's the definition of a public eyesore? To some it's an abandoned house, to others a junk heap. For many of the residents of Headington, a suburb of Oxford in England, it's Bill Hine's shark.

Bill decided to have a 25 ft fiberglass shark sculpted and displayed on his roof. He says it's his protest against man's inhumanity to man, specifically the use of atomic bombs. Many wanted it torn down, and the great shark debate raged for 6 years until 1992, when the Oxford town council, after hearing days of arguments on both sides, decided that for the council to discourage creativity and expression was contrary to Oxford's long history as an educational center of the world. So they found for Bill Hine and his shark, making it Headington's biggest fish out of water.

*The shark on
Bill Hine's roof is there to stay.*

Martha Washington, premier First Lady of the United States, made her silverware into currency. The Washington cutlery service was a source of the silver that went into the first US coins after the Revolution.

One of the most remarkable coincidences concerns *Futility*, a novel written by retired Merchant Navy officer Morgan Robertson. His story told of a mighty British liner, the fastest and most luxurious ever built, which set out on its maiden voyage from Southampton to New York. On it were 3,000 passengers. But the ship was doomed. Mid-Atlantic, the starboard side of the ship struck an iceberg and the vessel, advertised as 'unsinkable', sank with a huge loss of life – because there were not enough lifeboats. Morgan Robertson wrote his book in 1898.

In the early 20th century a real ocean liner set out on *her* maiden voyage from Southampton to New York. Mid-Atlantic the ship hit an iceberg and sank, taking with her 1,513 souls. Most of the deaths were the result of there being too few lifeboats. The real ship sank in the same spot Robertson described in *Futility*. On it were 3,000 passengers.

The ship which sank on April 14 1912 was called *The Titanic*. Morgan Robertson's imaginary ship, which he created 14 years earlier, was called *The Titan*.

The first tulip bulb was taken to Holland around 1550 from Turkey, where they grow wild. The importer planted it in his garden, where it was much admired. The tulip is the only flower which will suddenly produce a different variety of itself — almost as though it becomes bored with its appearance and decides to change just for the sake of changing.

When this happened for the first time in Holland, everybody wanted one of these fantastic flowers. The importer realized that the tulip could be a great commercial success, so he immediately increased the price. Tulip growers all over Holland began to develop different colors and the market expanded. The tulip became the subject of jealousy and disputes. Competitors began to sabotage each other's plants.

A huge black market developed and people began to mortgage their homes to borrow money in order to purchase the latest color. At the height of the 'battle' one collector exchanged 1,000 pounds of cheese, 4 oxen, 8 pigs, 12 sheep, a bed and a suit of clothes for a single bulb. But eventually and inevitably the market crashed. Thousands of people, including the aforementioned collector, were ruined. When the bottom fell out of the tulip market in 1637 the Dutch economy almost collapsed.

In 1986, the twentieth Fermat number $2^{2^{20}} + 1$ was tested on the Cray-2 supercomputer to see if it was a prime number. To answer this Yes-No question, the computer made billions of calculations. After 10 days, its answer was: NO!

Many people believe Charles Lindbergh was the first man to fly non-stop across the Atlantic in an airplane. In fact, Alcock and Brown, two British pilots, were the first to do so, flying from St John's, Newfoundland, to Clifden, Ireland, in a Vickers Vimy bomber in 1919.

More than 70 people flew across the Atlantic before Lindbergh. His achievement was that he was the first person to cross it non-stop *solo*.

*Britain's pilots Alcock and Brown took to the skies in 1919 and made a safe landing on the other side of the Atlantic.*

# Trivia

Pablo Diego José Francisco de Paula Juan Nepomuceno Crispin Crispiano de la Santisima Trinidad Ruiz y Picasso has a long name and an even longer list of artistic productions. He was the most prolific painter the world has ever seen. In a career that spanned 78 years, it is estimated that Picasso produced more than 13,500 paintings, 100,000 prints and engravings, 34,000 book illustrations and 300 sculptures. His life's work has been estimated to be worth over $800 million.

There is a club in the United States whose only membership requirement is that one has the name Jim Smith.

The foggy gray substance seen above a boiling pot and popularly referred to as steam is not, in fact, steam. It is the condensation that results from steam. Steam is that invisible area between the top of the pot or the end of the spout and the condensation.

**The eagle would not have been the United States' proud symbol if Benjamin Franklin had had his way. In 1789 he proposed to the Continental Congress that the eagle be scrapped as America's symbol, and replaced by another bird, a majestic, all-American bird. His nomination: the turkey.**

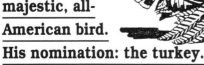

In 1992 IBM reported the biggest annual loss in its history – $4,965 billion. It represented a loss of $13.6 million per day, $566,781 every hour or $9,446 lost per minute.

People who want to plant notes to God in the Wailing Wall in Israel can now do it by fax. Every day hundreds of requests for divine intervention are stuffed into its cracks. Faxes sent to a number the phone company has set up will be brought to the wall by an employee. The number is not toll free.

In 1884 sock makers in Leicester, England, went on strike – for lower pay! They asked their employers to reduce their wages by 7.5 per cent because they thought they might get more work by being paid less. Their employers refused and they came out on strike. This was not the only example of striking for less: 40 years earlier coal miners in Durham and Northumberland petitioned not to be compelled to earn more than 3 shillings per day. When the managers refused, 80,000 men went on strike. No recent cases have been reported.

There really was a Robinson Crusoe, but his name was Alexander Selkirk. Associated with the buccaneer William Dampier, Selkirk, a Scotsman who lived from 1676 to 1721, was put ashore in 1704 on the uninhabited island of Juan Fernandez in the South Pacific following a quarrel. Juan Fernandez is about 300 miles off the coast of Chile. He stayed there for more than 4 years until he was rescued by a merchant ship. Selkirk told his story to Daniel Defoe, who subsequently wrote about the exploits in his novel *Robinson Crusoe*. There is a memorial on the island commemorating Selkirk's adventure.

As late as the 1850s a concoction of usnea and pieces of mummy was used as a treatment for nightmares. Usnea, as if you didn't know, is moss scraped from a criminal's skull. The worse the crime, the more potent the drug – so they used to say.

When performing surgery today, the last thing the doctor would want is for a handful of ants to fall on to the open wound. But in India and some areas of South America ancient physicians used to suture lacerations by placing large-clawed leaf-cutting ants on to the skin to hold the wound together. After the healing process began, the ants were twisted off and their claws eventually disintegrated.

It was a sad day for 20-year-old George when he fell in love. The object of his desire was young and shapely but it was an Austin Metro car! Reported in 1992 in *Sexual and Marital Therapy*, it was the first case of this rare fetish to be studied in Britain. George also liked the Vauxhall Nova, the Fiat Uno and the Ford Fiesta, but most of all he loved his Metro. He would drive for hours looking for spots where he could be alone with his car. A psychiatrist called in to help poor, love-lorn George said he was so attached to his car that he showed no interest in women, only becoming sexually aroused when he looked at his Metro. After months of reconditioning George's preferences have changed for the more ordinary: the opposite sex. Perhaps he will eventually find a wife named Mercedes.

Annie Wright Gregory died in 1943. Her father had been a drummer boy under George Washington at Valley Forge in 1777. Annie was born in 1843 when her father was in his eighties.

By entering into land deals with the British and allying with the monarchy before the American Revolution, the Mohicans managed to become one of America's most powerful Indian tribes after the Revolution. However, their success was short-lived and they were soon forced to agree to live on a reservation in southwestern Connecticut. The very last Mohican who could speak the Mohican language was Maq-Uua-pey, known to his neighbors as William Dick. He died in 1933. There are current-ly about 25 Mohicans living on the reservation. They are truly the Last of the Mohicans.

*The Mohicans were once one of America's most powerful Indian tribes. Few survive today.*

**AAA Septic Tank Service in California takes its business very seriously. Written on the side of their trucks is the legend: 'Your crap is our bread and butter'.**

# War stories

**The Great Wall of China was not, as one might expect, built to keep people out – attackers could easily find sectors of the wall which they could scale with little difficulty – but to keep the Hun's _horses_ from entering China. Without their horses, the Huns were an inefficient fighting force.**

The oldest event in world history that can be dated *exactly* was the peace treaty signed between the ancient armies of Media and Lydia in Asia Minor. The two armies were preparing for battle when a solar eclipse occurred. Shocked by the event as a sign from god that the impending war would be disastrous for both sides, the two signed their peace treaty. Astronomers have been able to fix the day as May 28, 585 BC.

After Union Army General Daniel E. Sickles had lost his leg to a cannonball at the Battle of Gettysburg, he sent both leg and cannonball to the Museum of Health and Medicine in Washington, DC. And how did he celebrate the anniversary of the battle? By visiting his leg, of course.

During World War II the construction of ice ships was taken very seriously. Cheaper than contemporary aircraft carriers, and quite possibly more buoyant, these weird ships, whose superstructures were to be carved entirely in ice, were to be used to transport troops and equipment across the Atlantic. According to the British Association for the Advancement of Science, 'Had not the atomic bomb been dropped on Japan and the war come to an end, ice ships would almost certainly have appeared on the oceans of the world.'

The Algerian ruler Dey Hussein was noted for his extremely bad temper. In 1830, during the course of an argument with the French Consul, he went too far. He slapped the Consul over the head with a fly swatter. War was declared, and Algeria subsequently became French territory.

A World War II destroyer once defeated a submarine with the help of a seldom-used weapon of destruction: potatoes. The USS *O'Bannon* was on patrol off the Solomon Islands in April 1943 when it encountered a Japanese sub. The crew shot off the sub's conning tower, preventing it from diving but then the captain of the sub brought it so close to the destroyer that the *O'Bannon*'s big guns could not be aimed at it. Nothing daunted, when the Japanese came topside, the gallant *O'Bannon* crewmen pelted them with potatoes. The Japanese thought they were being showered with grenades, threw their guns overboard, then panicked, submerged the sub and sank it. When the *O'Bannon* was decommissioned in the early 1970s, a plaque made to commemorate the event, and donated to the ship by the Maine potato growers, was taken to the Maine Maritime Museum. When a new ship was commissioned under the same name a few years later the plaque was transferred to it.

In occupied Holland during World War II, the Germans decided to fool the British by building a fake airfield. It was constructed meticulously but made almost entirely of wood. There were wooden hangars, oil tanks, gun emplacements, trucks and aircraft. But the Germans were so determined to make it look authentic that they took a little too long. Allied photographers observed their work, reported the hoax to headquarters and early one morning a lone RAF plane crossed the Channel, came in low, circled the completed 'airfield' once – and dropped a large wooden bomb.

British Intelligence were rather more successful with their hoaxes. They created a fake British Fourth Army for the benefit of German Counter-Intelligence. The area around Dover was made to look like a staging area for the invasion of the continent at Calais: it was equipped with rubber tanks, designed to resemble Sherman tanks, wooden gliders, aircraft and gun emplacements. To fool the German reconnaissance planes, dummy bomb craters were painted on large canvases – these came in two styles: one for sunny days and one for cloudy days, the difference being in the shadows they cast. When the canvases were placed on the ground, they were rotated periodically according to the position to the sun.

It was such a masterly deception that when the actual Normandy invasion took place the German generals thought that it was a diversionary tactic and that the actual invasion would still occur at Calais. Most of the camouflage work was done by set designers in English film studios.

*One of the British Army's secret weapons: a rubber lorry!*

# The last word

*Now try saying it!*

According to the Oxford English Dictionary the longest, non-name word in the English language is pneumonoultramicroscopicsilicovolcanoconiosises. It is the plural of the disease 'caused by the inhalation of very fine silica dust'. 'Sneeze' is a shorter word.

The term honeymoon, referring to the time period when the marriage consummation takes place, derives from the ancient northern European tradition of drinking honeyed wine as an aphrodisiac during the first month of marriage.

The most succinct word, according to the world's lexicographers, is the Fuegian 'mamihlapatapai'. It is used in the southernmost parts of Argentina and Chile and means 'looking at each other hoping that either will offer to do something which both parties desire but are unwilling to do'!